Christian Active Parenting

A Parent's Guide to Raising Children of Joy, Character and a Living Faith

MW00452766

ACTIVE PARENTING PUBLISHERS

Michael H. Popkin, PhD
Melody F. Popkin, and
Sue Allen, MA

©2015 Active Parenting Publishers. All rights reserved.

No part of this book may be reproduced in any form without written permission from the publisher.
Published by Active Parenting Publishers, Atlanta, Georgia.

ISBN: 978-1-59723-335-4

This book includes Scripture quotations from many different versions of the Holy Bible, which are listed below. These quotations are used with permission from the publishers or by the Fair Use Guidelines the publisher has cited.

CEV: Contemporary English Version © 1995 American Bible Society. All rights reserved.

ESV: English Standard Version © 2001 by Crossway, a publishing ministry of Good News Publishers. All rights reserved.

MSG: The Message © 1993, 1994, 1995, 1996, 2000, 2001, 2002. Used by permission of NavPress Publishing Group.

NIRV: New International Reader's Version © 1996, 1998 Biblica. All rights reserved throughout the world. Used by permission of Biblica.

NIV: New International Version © 1973, 1978, 1984, 2011 by Biblica, Inc. Used by permission. All rights reserved worldwide.

NKJV: New King James Version © 1982 by Thomas Nelson. Used by permission. All rights reserved.

NLT: New Living Translation © 1996, 2004, 2007 by Tyndale House Foundation. Used by permission of Tyndale House Publishers, Inc., Carol Stream, Illinois 60188. All rights reserved.

NRSV: New Revised Standard Version © 1989 the Division of Christian Education of the National Council of the Churches of Christ in the United States of America. Used by permission. All rights reserved.

RSV: Revised Standard Version © 1946, 1952, and 1971 the Division of Christian Education of the National Council of the Churches of Christ in the United States of America. Used by permission. All rights reserved.

DEDICATIONS

From Michael and Melody Popkin:

To our parents, Margie and John Fulford, Mona, Naomi and Harry Popkin
To our children, Megan and Ben Popkin

From Sue Allen:

To my parents, Tom and Marie Herr
To my husband, Steve
To our children, Kyler, Tessa, Adrianna, and Jeremiah

"I am reminded of your sincere faith, a faith that lived first in your grandmother Lois and your mother Eunice and now, I am sure, lives in you."

2 Timothy 1:5 (NRSV)

A special acknowledgement goes to my mother, Margie Greenhaw Fulford. With her sincere faith, she nurtured the love of Christ in our family. Her incredible parenting skills matched Active Parenting even before we knew there was parenting education. Though Mom was not alive when Megan and Ben were born, she has had great influence on how they were parented. I carry in my heart her unconditional love, support, loyalty and faith teaching, which inspired much of my writing and input in Christian Active Parenting. An early supporter of Active Parenting, she felt a kindred spirit to its cause. Mom, "Aunt Margie" to many, was the center of our family, including her brothers, sisters (she always said her sisters in law were truly her sisters), nieces, and nephews. She uplifted us all with her strength, constancy, faith, and love, but the greatest of these was her love, which lives on today.

- Melody Popkin

Photo provided by my dear friend Lynn.

Table of Contents

About The Authors

MICHAEL H. POPKIN, PhD, founder of Active Parenting Publishers and author of more than two dozen books and video programs on parenting, has been empowering parents to empower their children for over 30 years. He and his wife, Melody, live and work together in Atlanta and are the parents of two young adult children.

Building upon Dr. Popkin's work, co-authors Melody Popkin and Sue Allen have harnessed the power of their living faith to produce this Christian edition of the widely respected and highly successful *Active Parenting 4th Edition Parent's Guide*.

MELODY F. POPKIN is Manager of Christian Resources at Active Parenting Publishers, where she works alongside her husband, Michael. Melody's background in software training combined with her deep devotion to Christianity and faith studies inspired her to bring a Christian perspective to the Active Parenting program.

SUE ALLEN, MA, holds a master's degree in Human Development and Family Relations. She is the Director of Women's Discipleship at Northside Church in Atlanta. Seeking to share God's love and inspiration with others, Sue has self-published numerous Christian books and writes a daily blog encouraging many in their walk of faith. She and her husband are parents of four faith-filled children.

Acknowledgements

Christian Active Parenting was developed from the foundation of Active Parenting 4th Edition, which is largely based on the theories of Alfred Adler and Rudolf Dreikurs, two of the truly great psychological thinkers of the 20th Century. Their principles and methods, proven effective with millions of parents and educators, work in unity with the tenets and Scriptures of Christian faith to make Christian Active Parenting (CAP).

To complement the Adlerian base of the material, we have included work derived from communication theorists such as Tom Gordon, Carl Rogers, and Robert Carkuff. The combination of empathy training, Adlerian parenting methods, and biblical references represents a powerful Christian parenting model that can be taught to all parents living in a democratic society (or an emerging democratic society).

While updating the Active Parenting model to reflect Christian faith, we were fortunate to have the input of an experienced and talented advisory board comprised of faith-based family service professionals and parents. Each of them gave us input and feedback that made this a much better program. We are indebted to this group of dedicated individuals who gave of their time and talents.

We also gathered input from parents nationwide who wrote to us about their daily conflicts, as well as from Active Parenting class leaders who shared methods and stories gleaned from years of experience. Their support of parent education is lived every day in hundreds of behind-the-scenes ways. Their lives became the basis of many of the stories you'll read in this book.

We would like to thank Dr. G. Gil Watson, Senior Pastor at Northside United Methodist Church in Atlanta, Georgia, for his inspirational sermons and the Women's Ministry at Northside for opening their doors to us and hosting the first CAP test group. It gave us valuable feedback as we began this project four years ago. Thank you to Dr. Charles F. Stanley of First Baptist Church Atlanta and Pastor Charles Andrew (Andy) Stanley of North Point Community Church for the inspiration provided through their messages.

A huge acknowledgement and appreciation goes to the Product Development Department at Active Parenting: Manager Molly Davis shepherded this project from start to finish. Her dedication to making this the best Christian parenting program available is without measure. We are indebted to Molly for her understanding and loyalty to the project. Art Director Gabrielle Tingley created a vibrant look for the program, and Coordinator Rhea Lewis-Ngcobo supported us with patience and adaptability. The entire staff at APP contributed in countless ways, small and large. Our programs are truly a company-wide effort.

We are grateful for our children, Megan and Ben Popkin, who give us the love, support and experience to create a program with faith. You are using the gifts God gave you and thriving as independent and interdependent adults in this democratic society in which we live. We love you more than can be measured.

We are grateful for our friends who listened to, supported, and prayed for us during these last three years as we researched and wrote Christian Active Parenting. You continue to teach us the power of prayer.

We are grateful to God for his presence through the process and for sending us Sue to help bring this dream to fruition.

Dr. Michael and Melody Popkin

With deep gratitude, I thank my husband and gifted best friend, Steve. With you, the adventure of daily life is fun and meaningful. Collaborating together, we enjoy supporting our four children, Kyler, Tessa, Adrianna, and Jeremiah. I marvel at the uniquely talented people God is sparking you each to become. As a family, may we continue to fan these sparks into flame, generation after generation.

I am also grateful for the spiritual friendships that nurture me day by day. Each walk-and-talk, each meal shared, and each encouraging word from you awakens more of me. Thank you, my loving friends.

How wise God is to knit my spiritual gifts together with those of Michael and Melody. For our lifelong bond, I am forever grateful.

Sue Allen

"The Lord said, 'I will bless you

… with wisdom, with strength, with a sturdy faith to sustain your family.

and you will be a blessing

… to your children, to their children, to the generations who follow. And eventually …

All the families on Earth will be blessed through you.'"

With this blessing, God's loving kindness fills your home and overflows into the world around you.

Genesis 12:2a-b (NLT)

Transcribed from Gerardo Davila's narration as host of the Christian Active Parenting video

Introduction

Christian Active Parenting (CAP) is designed to equip families to thrive by teaching parents practical skills grounded in the wisdom of Scripture. CAP is based on the proven parenting skills in *Active Parenting 4th Edition* by Dr. Michael Popkin. When Dr. Popkin founded Active Parenting Publishers in 1980, he was a child and family therapist at a local hospital where he also provided parent education and counseling. He saw firsthand that effective parenting methods could change the lives of parents and children. This led him to develop the *Active Parenting Discussion Program*, the world's first video-based parenting education program. Since then, Active Parenting books and courses have helped over three million parents in countries all over the world communicate more clearly, strengthen relationships with their children, and bring harmony to their families' lives.

The idea for *Christian Active Parenting* began in 2011 after we heard feedback from parents who were taking the *Active Parenting Now* course at our local church. They wanted to integrate their faith into the practical parenting methods they were learning. We began adding biblical thought and Scripture to the course, and soon the idea of developing a full program began to take shape. After much prayer and thought, we began writing *Christian Active Parenting*.

When we chose to develop our Christian program on the foundation of *Active Parenting 4th Edition*, it was with a deep appreciation of that program's ability to bring joy back into parenting, a goal that resonated with us not only as parents but also as Christians. Joy is a natural byproduct of a living faith in our all-powerful, ever-present God. As Nehemiah 8:10b (NIV) encourages: "...the joy of the Lord is your strength." In times of trouble, happiness may abandon us, but joy will remain, steady and strong, a force that rises up above all adversity. Weaving CAP methods into the fabric of Christian families, we hope to make room for more joy in the hearts of parents and children alike.

A second goal for CAP was to help parents raise children of strong Christian character. CAP methods are designed to develop within each child an inner compass and an ability to stick to doing the right thing when faced with life challenges. Day after day, "endurance produces character, and character produces hope" (Romans 5:4, ESV). Encouraging parents to successfully establish CAP methods at home, we believe, will eventually send into society young people who will positively impact the world around them.

Our third motivation for writing this program was to pass along our living faith in God. When we as parents put our living faith into action, God strengthens our families. When we parent actively out of our reservoir of living faith, we spark a living faith in our children. Through faith, our children's Christian character grows stronger. God blesses parents with a living faith; parents pass the blessing on to their children; the children develop their own living faith and pass the blessing on to their own families and to the world at large.

> "It's in Christ that we find out who we are and what we are living for.
> Long before we first heard of Christ ... he had his eye on us, had designs on us for glorious living, part of the overall purpose he is working out in everything and everyone."
> *Ephesians 1:11-12 (MSG)*

We wish you the same success millions of parents have experienced with Active Parenting methods over the years. Enjoy your journey to discover how *Christian Active Parenting* can help you raise children of joy, character, and a living faith. As you bless your children, they will become a blessing to the world.

Melody Popkin and Sue Allen

1: The Christian Active Parent

*"Train up a child in the way he should go,
and when he is old he will not depart from it."*

Proverbs 22:6 (RSV)

To parent our children well and to live as faithful Christians: these may be the two highest callings we have as human beings. Of course, we want to do both to the best of our abilities and because they are such important goals, we don't want to shortchange either of them. Both are important to us and our children. Both are interdependent and connected.

To succeed, we will need to train ourselves not only by learning new parenting skills but also by strengthening and depending on our relationship with God.

The ageless wisdom captured in Proverbs 22:6 provides a good starting point as we begin looking at the connection between Christian faith and our role as parents. These words, though straightforward, are not to suggest that it is an easy task to "train up" children. The dictionary defines the verb "to train" as "to teach a particular skill or type of behavior through practice and instruction over a period of time." What skills and behavior should we be teaching our children? And how can these lessons mesh with Christian faith? "Training up" a child is not easy, but we as parents should be committed to the goal of guiding our children in "the way they should go." To succeed, we will need to train ourselves not only by learning new parenting skills but also by strengthening and depending on our relationship with God. Most importantly, we'll need to fuse our faith and our role as parents to gain the outcome we desire.

Perhaps the truest thing that can be said about parenting is that it requires a lot of time and energy. It is a tremendously "active" undertaking, requiring a 24/7 commitment with a tool chest of skills ranging from discipline to communication and support. Because children respond better to actions than to words, to be an effective parent is to be an active parent. This helps explain the "Active" in *Christian Active Parenting.*

We also think of the word "active" as a contrast to the "reactive" (or sometimes just *in*active) approach used by most parents. Reactive parents wait until their children push them to their limits, and then they react. Often they react with frustration, anger, and random discipline — or as one mother put it, "the screech and hit" school of parenting. When parents "react" rather than "act," or when they don't act at all, they allow the child to control both the situation and the parent's emotions. Problems tend to continue or even get worse as parent and child play out the same frustrating scenes over and over.

> *When parents "react" rather than "act," or when they don't act at all, they allow the child to control both the situation and the parent's emotions.*

Part of the problem is that most parents do not have a consistent approach to parenting. They use a little of what their parents did, a little of the exact opposite of what their parents did, and a little of what they picked up from friends, books, and the Internet. Our philosophy in *Christian Active Parenting* (CAP) is that it is the job of the parent, with God's help, to play the leadership role in the family. CAP will help you establish goals for your child and teach you effective methods for leading your child toward those goals. It will also teach you a consistent model of parenting, enabling you to act with confidence and clarity as you encounter the many challenges parents face.

A word of caution: Through this book, you will learn a very practical model for understanding and leading children. This model has been used effectively by millions of parents, counselors, teachers, and psychologists. It works! However, it is put into use by human beings, and human beings, as we all know, are imperfect. We make mistakes. As you make your way through this book you will probably become aware of two kinds of mistakes of your own:

First, you may realize or recall mistakes you have made in your own parenting. Almost everyone does. It is helpful to recognize these mistakes and learn from them. But it is also important to let them go. They are in the past, and it is useless to dwell on them now. It's much more productive to concentrate on being a more effective parent in the present and in the future!

Second, you will make further mistakes as you learn these new skills. Mistakes are part of the learning process, and they happen to everyone using new skills. So it is important that you accept your mistakes without punishing yourself for being imperfect. If you are too hard on yourself, you not only make yourself feel bad, but you also put limits on your learning. This is because when we feel criticized, even by ourselves, we become defensive. Soon we don't even admit our mistakes to ourselves, and we lose a valuable opportunity to correct and improve our performance. Taking your mistakes to God, who shows mercy to us all, will relieve the burden. Proverbs 28:13 (NLT) reassures us, "People who conceal their sins will not prosper, but if they confess and turn from them, they will receive mercy." So, learn to catch yourself with a smile instead of a kick and you will learn more, feel better, and see change faster.

Learn to catch yourself with a smile instead of a kick and you will learn more, feel better, and see change faster.

The Parent's Affirmation of Imperfection

"I accept that I am an imperfect parent, that I have made mistakes in the past, and that I will make mistakes in the future.

I will lay down my mistakes before God and will not hide them or pretend that I am perfect. Nor will I beat myself up over them. Instead, I will catch my mistakes — with a smile instead of a kick — and learn what I can from them. This will help me avoid making the same mistake too often as I become a better parent.

My goal is to be a very good and faithful parent, perhaps even an excellent one. But I will never be a perfect parent, and that's OK, because my children are better off with an imperfect parent who can teach them the value of learning from their own mistakes."

God accepts us as imperfect parents, understanding that we have made mistakes in the past and will make more mistakes in the future. Why try to hide our flaws from God or pretend to be perfect with one another? When we fall short, we can look to God's forgiving grace. Instead of striving for perfection, we strive to make progress daily, with the help of God's Holy Spirit in our hearts. Following our example, our children will learn the value of admitting their own mistakes.

Imperfect as we are, we would do well to remember the encouraging words of Peter: "Above all, love each other deeply, because love covers over a multitude of sins." (1 Peter 4:8, NIV) Just as God graciously loves, accepts, and guides us as imperfect parents, we love our children the best way we know how: we accept them, we guide them, and we show them the grace of forgiveness.

> **"Forgetting the past and looking forward to what lies ahead, I press on to reach the end of the race and receive the heavenly prize for which God, through Christ Jesus, is calling us."**
>
> *Philippians 3:13-14 (NLT)*

Mary, Mother of Jesus

As we begin to explore what it means to be both a Christian and a good parent, it is fitting that we honor one of the Bible's greatest parents: Mary, the mother of Jesus. Mary heard the angel Gabriel's pronouncement that she, a virgin, would bear a son, and "the holy one to be born will be called the Son of God" Luke 1:35, (NIV), and she leaned into her faith, believing that God was with her. Arriving in Bethlehem and finding a warm and safe place for the Son of God to be born, Mary and Josepsh welcomed Jesus. Mary's was the first face He saw, trusted, and loved. Her love and care as a mother produced a young man whose faith and loyalty to God were beyond measure: the only perfect human. He would come to fulfill God's will, using His gifts to change the world through the power of love, but first He had to grow from infant to child to a thriving independent adult. Mary and Joseph were the ones who raised Him, fed Him, clothed Him. and most certainly encouraged Him to follow God's will. The importance of Mary's role in our Christian faith is hard to overstate, and there is much we can learn from the example she set as a parent.

Parenting: The Most Important Job

Parenting, though still one of the most underrated jobs in our society, is beginning to attract some of the attention and consideration it deserves. After all, if the future of our society is our children, then the key to that future rests primarily with parents and teachers. Many schools, religious institutions, social service centers, and other community organizations are responding to this responsibility by offering support to parents through programs such as *Christian Active Parenting*.

The Purpose of Parenting

> **"Children are a gift from the Lord."**
>
> *Psalm 127:3 (CEV)*

Children truly are a gift from God. They will bring much joy to our lives. But the job of parenting is a difficult one. Success at any job first requires a sound understanding of its purpose. The basic purpose of parenting has not changed throughout history. We can state it like this:

> *The purpose of parenting is to protect and prepare children to survive and thrive in the kind of society in which they live.*

All parents have beliefs and values that influence how and why they go about achieving this purpose, though some might not be conscious of it. As Christian parents, our faith is integral to our purpose and cannot be separated. In John 10:10b (AMP), Jesus reveals His hope for all of us: "I came that they may have and enjoy life, and have it in abundance (to the full, till it overflows)." God designed us, and our children, to go beyond simply surviving to joyfully thriving. Therefore, Christian parenting deserves its own purpose statement, one that reflects how the twin callings of Christian faith and parenting are completely and harmoniously intertwined within it:

> *The purposes of Christian parenting are to protect and prepare our children with God's loving grace to survive and thrive in the society in which they live, following the example of Jesus Christ through the power of the Holy Spirit.*

Throughout this book we will turn to the Bible for support and inspiration to help us fulfill our important purpose as Christian parents. We read in 2 Timothy 3:16-17 (NIV) that "All Scripture is God-breathed and is useful for teaching, rebuking, correcting, and training in righteousness, so that the servant of God may be thoroughly equipped for every good work." As we put into practice Active Parenting skills enlightened by biblical truths, the power of the Holy Spirit will equip us to do God's good, hard work as Christian Active Parents. Raising children of joy, character, and a living faith is certainly worth our efforts.

Why Christian Families Need Active Parenting More Than Ever

The society in which we live has changed through the years. For example:

In some ways, it is more dangerous. The illegal and prescription drugs available to today's children and teens are easier to find and more harmful than ever. Crimes against children — and crimes by children — are more numerous than when we were growing up. There is a serious problem with violence in schools and the risk of terrorism now concerns us all. In other areas, it has become safer. For example, the medical, mental health, and social sciences are finding better ways to combat addictions and improve health; smoking has been banned in public areas; civil rights are more universally recognized; ecumenicalism and interfaith prayer have been established; and we have a better understanding of the interconnectedness of the entire human community.

The increased dangers pose a challenge for parents. Part of our purpose is to protect our children so they will survive. Yet if we overprotect them, we are not preparing them to survive and thrive on their own. Keep in mind that the job of parenting is to work you out of a job! After all, the plan is for our kids to leave home someday and to survive us by many days. That means preparing your child for independence in a world full of increasing opportunities. Three things will help you do this:

1. Talk with other adults to get an idea of what risks are reasonable for your child to take in your community. For example, how old should they be when they're left home alone, and where is it safe for them to play?

2. Join with other parents at your child's school, in your church family, in ecumenical and interfaith groups, and through other organizations in your community to make it a better place to rear children. Get involved. Be active. You, your family, and your community will all benefit.

3. Allow your child to develop independence gradually. *Christian Active Parenting* will help you learn the skills that will encourage your child to build independence. Because children develop through various stages, appropriate behavior at one age may not be appropriate at another. There are many good books available to help you know what to expect at these ages and stages of development. Talking with other parents and your child's teachers will help, too.

Society is more diverse and more just. If the bad news about modern society is that it has become more dangerous, the good news is that it has also become more just. We can be proud that our country was founded on the principle that all people are created equal. In fact, this concept of equality is a hallmark of democratic societies throughout the world.

Unfortunately, the word "all" in the United States of 1776 really meant all white males who owned land. The rest were not even allowed to vote. But the ball of social progress was moving, and during the next 150 years, such milestones as the end of slavery, the beginning of the labor movement, and the right of women to vote showed that we intended to fulfill the promise of democracy. Then, in the 1950s with the advent of television, the movement for social equality took a giant leap forward. When Martin Luther King, Jr. spoke of his dream of equality for all humankind, television was there to carry his message throughout the world. The Civil Rights Movement brought real change — to our laws, to our attitudes about other people, and to our expectations about what kind of people can succeed. One group after another began to demand that they, too, be treated as equals. The 1990s saw the mushrooming of the worldwide Web. Its impact on social equality is without peer. No other medium has been as effective at leveling the playing field as the Internet. Today, no group accepts being treated as inferior, unquestioningly doing what they are told, or speaking only when spoken to.[1]

> *Today's children will not put up with being "seen and not heard" or otherwise treated disrespectfully.*

The atmosphere of equality in which our children live has created a challenge for today's parents. We must now contend with a generation of children who are no longer comfortable with the traditional child's role of inferiority in society. Today's children will not put up with being "seen and not heard" or otherwise treated disrespectfully.

The methods taught in this book take into account the need for new approaches to leadership in a society of equals. However, the concept that "all (people) are created equal" does not mean that all people are created the same. Differences between people range from the obvious, such as how we look, to the subtle, such as our dreams and values. People also have different roles to play in society and different responsibilities that come with these roles. A passage from Corinthians recognizes each of us as unique individuals who are gifted by God:

---

[1]   Active Parenting was first published in the United States, and the historical references in this guide tend to center around this democratic society. But each democratic society has its own stories to tell. Parents in countries other than the U.S. may wish to use examples from their own history about their struggle for equality.

"There are different kinds of service, but we serve the same Lord. God works in different ways, but it is the same God who does work in all of us. A spiritual gift is given to each of us so we can help each other." (1 Corinthians 12:5-7, NLT) As we uncover our own spiritual gifts and the unique spiritual gifts of our children, we help serve and support each other just as our family serves the Lord.

In spite of these differences, we are each considered of equal value and worth under our Constitution. This means we are entitled to equal protection under the law; equal opportunity for employment; an equal right to make our opinions known; and an equal right to be treated respectfully, to name a few.

A major way that parents and children are still different is in the roles they play. The parent's role is that of the leader, while the child more often plays the role of the learner.

Likewise, in a family, parents and children are equal in some ways and different in others. A major way that parents and children are still different is in the roles they play. The parent's role is that of the leader, while the child more often plays the role of the learner. As the leaders in the family, parents have certain rights and responsibilities that differ from those of their children. For example, we have the responsibility of providing food, clothing, shelter, and protection for our children. We also have the right to drive, vote, use alcohol, and exercise other privileges that are not available to children.

In addition, we have the authority to decide many of the matters that affect the lives of our children, including matters of health, safety, and family values. Since this includes how we decide to parent, we will look at the concept of authority more closely later in the chapter.

Society changes at an increasing rate. Today's high-tech society changes faster than any in history. Jobs and even industries that thrive in one decade may be gone the next, replaced by new technologies that were undiscovered when we were in school. Never before has media been able to penetrate our lives more thoroughly through TV, Internet, smartphones, etc. as it does today. Success in such a rapidly changing society requires children to do much more than just learn new skills. They must also learn how to adapt to change and keep learning.

Neither blind obedience nor an attitude of complacency is likely to provide them with the skills and character necessary to navigate the current of change that is likely to come. This book will teach you methods for empowering your children to be decision makers, problem solvers, team players, and lifelong learners, regardless of what career paths they may choose.

Family make-up has changed. Change in society has also affected the very make-up of families. The traditional family of two biological parents and children is no longer the norm. More than half of all children will find themselves in single parent families or families blended together with parents and children from previous marriages. Many other children will live with grandparents, same sex parents, or other caregivers with whom they share no previous ties at all. No matter what type of family you have, the skills in this book will help you develop the kind of relationship you and your child need to thrive now and in the future.

We need God's power to face the mountain of challenges that life sets before us..

We need God's power to face the mountain of challenges that life sets before us. Fortunately, 1 John 4:4 (NLT) promises: "… the Spirit who lives in you is greater than the spirit who lives in the world." On our behalf, Jesus prayed: "Father, I don't ask you to take my followers out of the world, but keep them safe from the evil one. They don't belong to this world, and neither do I. Your word is the truth. So let this truth make them completely yours. I am sending them into the world, just as you sent me." Tapping into God's Spirit that lives within us, we will adapt and learn to thrive in our ever-changing society.

The Risks: Drugs, Sexuality, and Violence

The risks associated with drugs, sexuality, and violence are greatest during the teen years. However, what you do now as parents will make a huge difference in what your children will do later when you are not around. The skills you will learn in this book will focus on four major ways to help you reduce the risk that your children will become harmfully involved in these three areas:

1. Build character and develop skills in your child.

The Christian Active Parenting skills are designed to help build six important qualities of character: faith, courage, self-esteem, responsibility, cooperation, and respect. You will learn ways to instill these characteristics in your children and help them develop the personal skills that they will need to succeed, including skills for problem solving, communication, anger management, and academic success. By developing these characteristics and success skills, we give our children a strong foundation from which to resist easy answers to life's problems, such as tobacco, alcohol and other drugs, reckless sexuality, and violence.

The Active model of parenting focuses specifically on strengthening the parent-child relationship, which both minimizes the likelihood of rebellion and enables you to influence your child more effectively.

Research supports this approach. The Search Institute has identified a list of 40 Developmental Assets that are key to preventing negative outcomes in child and youth development. These assets include commitments, values, competencies, and self-perceptions that, if nurtured within young people, provide them with "internal compasses" to guide their behaviors and choices. You will find a list of 40 Developmental Assets in Addendum II.

2. Build a strong relationship with your child.

A powerful message about relationships can be found in Paul's teachings to the people of the church in Corinth: "If I speak in the tongues of men or of angels, but do not have love, I am only a resounding gong or a clanging cymbal. If I have the gift of prophesy and can fathom all mysteries and all knowledge, and if I have a faith that can move mountains, but do not have love, I am nothing" (1 Corinthians 13:1-2, NIV). This wisdom continues in verse 13:13, "And now these three remain: faith, hope, and love. But the greatest of these is love."

Our ability to influence the values our children form and the decisions they make is, to a large extent, dependent on the quality of our relationship with them. Starting from a place of love, we can begin to develop a strong bond. If the relationship is mostly negative, they often reject even our good ideas. They are quick to rebel to show us that we can't push them around. As the teen years approach, this rebellion is more likely to involve drug use, sexuality, and violence, as our children intentionally reject our values in these matters. The Active model of parenting focuses specifically on strengthening the parent-child relationship, which both minimizes the likelihood of rebellion and enables you to influence your child more effectively.

3. Talk persuasively about the risks.

Once you have established a positive relationship with your child, it is important to talk about the specific risks involved with drugs, sexuality, and violence. You want to be as persuasive as possible in making your case and winning over your child's attitude, because ultimately it will be up to him or her to decide what to do when confronted with these risks. Discipline can be helpful, but discipline alone is not enough to win the battle for a child's mind. We will discuss effective communication skills in Chapter 2, encouragement and self-esteem in Chapter 4, and the use of family meetings throughout this guide.

4. Filter out negative influences in your child's life.

You can't be with your children every minute of the day, but that doesn't mean you can't be a major influence in their everyday lives. God empowers us to act as filters for our children, letting in the people and experiences that nurture developmental and spiritual growth, and shutting out influences that hinder or stall their growth. To mature into faithful, influential members of our society, our children need us to protect and support the growth of their unique characters.

Do You Have a Spirited Child?

Some children are born with a temperament that is more spirited and challenging than others, presenting special challenges to parents, teachers, and others who live and work with them. Spirited children have traditionally been subjected to negative labeling. From "defiant and strong-willed" to "obstinate and defiant," there is always the implication that something is wrong at their core and must be corrected. But "spirit" is really a high-risk, high-reward proposition: The five qualities that make these kids a challenge to manage (heightened curiosity, adventure, power, persistence, and sensitivity) are the same qualities that can make them highly productive, fruitful human beings — even champions.

If you suspect that you have a spirited child, please understand that you did not make him this way. Temperament, whether it's shyness, extroversion, or anything else, is part of a child's DNA. You are not to blame, nor do you get any credit. On the other hand, how you parent a spirited nature can make a big difference in how your child uses that spirit. The skills you will be learning in this book can be used to help "tame" (not "break") your child's spirited nature so that she learns to use it constructively. It will take more time and patience than with other children, and you will want to consult other resources and look for help where you can find it. But stick with it and the pay-off that comes from seeing your child learn to manage his emotions and use his God-given assets to thrive will be well worth the effort.

Dr. Popkin's book *Taming the Spirited Child (New York: Simon and Schuster)* is also available from Active Parenting Publishers.

The Substance Abuse and Mental Health Services Administration of the U.S. government (SAMHSA) has identified certain risk factors that our children face in today's society as well as the corresponding protective factors that we can provide and develop to counteract these risks. You will find a complete list in Addendum I. In Chapter 6, we will see some practical ways that you can act as a "filter" to screen out risks, while also encouraging positive influences for your child.

What We Can Learn from a 17th-Century Swedish Battleship

Ballast is the core values that you can help instill in your children—the stable character they will need to make good decisions throughout their lives when the waves get high and the winds blow hard.

In 1628, Sweden built one of the world's greatest battleships to date, the *Wasa*. The feature that made this ship so formidable was an upper deck of cannons in addition to the usual first deck. As the day of its launch grew near, the people of Stockholm, from nobles to townspeople, became more and more excited to see the mighty ship set sail. Finally, the day of its christening arrived and the *Wasa* took to the seas, hit a storm scarcely a mile out of the harbor, rolled over, and sank. The problem wasn't so much the storm — after all, other ships had withstood far worse storms. The problem was that the *Wasa* didn't have enough weight in its hull, or *ballast*, to counter the heavy upper row of cannons and stabilize itself. Lacking the proper ballast, the *Wasa* was no match for the storm's winds and waves. It simply toppled over and went down like a stone.

Here is an interesting second definition of *ballast*: "That which gives stability to character." Ballast is the core values that you can help instill in your children — the stable character they will need to make good decisions throughout their lives when the waves get high and the winds blow hard.

Three Kinds of Character

The concept of character is going to come up again and again in this book. It's a cornerstone of the CAP philosophy. But what *is* character, and where does it fit into the bigger picture of helping our children to survive and thrive? First, it is helpful to recognize that when we speak of character, we are really talking about three different things. The first might be something like this:

> *Character is the sum total of a person's values, beliefs, attitudes, actions, and personality traits.*

This is what we mean when we speak of a person's "character." Is he courageous or cowardly? Can you count on her or not? Does he possess such qualities as honesty, responsibility, perseverance, cooperativeness, and respect? When we hear the term "character education," it usually refers to efforts to instill these and other qualities of positive character in children. We will be learning methods of instilling such qualities throughout this book, because these qualities enable our children to survive and thrive in our modern society.

This positive type of character is usually good for the child, the family, and the community. However, it is also possible in our society to have high self-esteem, courage, and many other positive character traits and yet still choose to break the rules, live outside the law, and otherwise reject the limits of society. This is why it is also important for our children to develop a second type of character:

> *Character is the courage to do the right thing even when you could get away with doing the wrong thing, or when doing the right thing may cause you to lose something you want.*

Many people in our society only obey the law because they fear punishment if they break the law and get caught. This is not character; it's fear. These same people would break the law if they thought they could get away with it. In fact many rules, laws, and norms of morality are broken every day by people who think they can get away with it, and often they do. Truth be told, most of us fall short of this definition of character at times. It is a difficult goal to attain. However, it is a worthy goal to work toward, and one worth instilling in our children. After all, we won't always be there looking over their shoulders. If we have not instilled in them the values and beliefs of good character — the integrity to do the right thing just because they believe it is the right thing to do — then no amount of discipline or rewards is going to be sufficient. Eventually they will succumb to the temptation to break the rules and the pressure to take an easy path to feeling good about themselves. In today's society this means harmful involvement with tobacco, alcohol, and other drugs, reckless sexuality, violence, and other dangerous and hurtful behaviors.

The third type of character, growing in our lives as believers, is Christian character.

> *Christian character is the result of the Holy Spirit's work in the heart of a person, to develop the fruits of the spirit as God's way of living out the teachings of Jesus Christ.*

As Christian parents, we seek to live and shepherd our children in God's ways. Galatians 5:22-23 (MSG) describes how this maturing process affects our lives: "But what happens when we live God's way? God brings gifts into our lives, much the same way that fruit appears in an orchard — things like affection for others, exuberance about life, serenity. We develop a willingness to stick with things, a sense of compassion in the heart, and a conviction that a basic holiness permeates things and people. We find ourselves involved in loyal commitments, not needing to force our way in life, able to marshal and direct our energies wisely."

Over time, just as a well-tended orchard produces fruit, our Christian faith produces fruits of the Spirit. The New Living Translation interpretation of Galatians 5:22 explains: "But the Holy Spirit produces this kind of fruit in our lives: love, joy, peace, patience, kindness, goodness, faithfulness, gentleness, and self-control." With faith in God and our own nurturing as parents, we can help the qualities of Christian character take root and grow in our children's hearts.

How Bobby Jones Chose Character Over Victory

There is a famous story about the golf legend Bobby Jones. He was playing in the 1925 U.S. Open when his ball came to rest on the side of a hill. As he placed his club down to begin his stroke, the ball moved slightly, a violation of a golf rule calling for a one-stroke penalty. Though nobody but him saw the ball move, and it had not given him an advantage, he assessed himself the penalty. He lost the tournament by one stroke in a playoff. Although praised by many sports writers for his gesture, Jones was reported to have said, "You might as well praise me for not robbing banks."

The character that Jones showed by doing the right thing when he could have gotten away with doing the wrong thing was a quality that stood him well his entire life. It didn't matter that he lost the tournament. He would have done the same thing even if he had known it would cause him to lose. We know this because at the next year's U.S. Open a similar thing happened. A strong wind moved his ball on the putting green after he had placed his club behind it to begin his putt. Again nobody but Jones noticed, and again he assessed himself the one-stroke penalty called for by the rules of golf. The fact that he went on to win the Open that year is less important than the character he again demonstrated with the choice he made.

What qualities of character do you want for your child?

Since our purpose of parenting is "to protect and prepare children with God's loving grace to survive and thrive as Christians in the kind of society in which they will live", we have to ask ourselves what it takes to survive and thrive in a fast paced, high tech, multi-cultural democracy. Do we want people who will unquestioningly do as they're told, who are blindly obedient and fearful of authority? That might be useful if we were raising our children to live under a dictatorship, but such qualities would not lead to success in a modern democratic society. Do we want to raise our children to make their own rules and do as they want? This might be useful if they lived in a lawless society, but under our rule of law, such people often end up in prison — or dead.

There are many qualities of character that are important for surviving and thriving in a democratic society, but six in particular seem to form the foundation upon which other qualities are built. These six qualities of character will be the ballast in your child's ship that will keep him steady as he sets out into the world of school, peer relations, and more.

Faith

Children who are rooted in a living faith are empowered to thrive amid life's myriad challenges.

As Christians, we put our faithful trust in God the Father, in Jesus the Son, and in the Holy Spirit alive in our hearts. As parents, our faith grounds our family and upholds the value of Christian character, supported by a conviction that is so aptly described in Hebrews 11:1 (MSG): "The fundamental fact of existence is that this trust in God, this faith, is the firm foundation under everything that makes life worth living." This is what we call a *living faith*. Children who are rooted in a living faith are empowered to thrive amid life's myriad challenges.

Courage

A free society provides many opportunities for people to succeed, but success is not guaranteed, nor is it easy to attain. Those who have the confidence to take worthwhile risks have the best chance to thrive. And when life gets tough, those with the courage and grit to persevere are more likely to succeed. We are told in Deuteronomy 31:6 (NLT): "So be strong and courageous! Do not be afraid and do not panic … For the Lord your God will personally go ahead of you. He will neither fail you nor abandon you."

Even among children, it takes great courage to resist peer pressure, to stand up for oneself or for others, to think independently, and to handle the many challenges of school. From the French word *coeur*, meaning heart, courage is a child's inner strength, necessary to withstand the fear that so often nips at self-esteem. We will focus on ways to instill this fundamental quality in Chapters 2 and 4.

Responsibility

Responsibility — a crucial concept in parenting — is the ability to recognize one's obligations, to know right from wrong, and to accept the consequences of one's decisions. Responsibility is a concept deeply rooted in Christian faith: "… God's law is not something alien, imposed on us from without, but woven into the very fabric of our creation. There is something deep within them that echoes God's yes and no, right and wrong." (Romans 2:15, MSG)

Many of the choices your child makes in the next few years may affect their entire lives.

Once children learn to take responsibility for their choices by experiencing the consequences that follow, they are equipped to make better choices. Many of the choices your child makes in the next few years may affect their entire lives. They will be offered tobacco, alcohol, and other drugs, and they will choose to accept or decline. They will face choices about sex, about dropping out of school, about work and careers, and perhaps even about whether to commit crimes. You won't be there, telling them what to do, but if you have helped to develop in them a personal relationship with God, if you have prepared them to make responsible decisions and instilled in them the courage to stand behind those decisions, they will be prepared to meet life's challenges. We will explore methods of teaching responsibility throughout this book, and especially in Chapter 3.

Cooperation

A child who learns to live and work cooperatively with others has a much better chance to succeed than the lone wolf or the rebel. As Matthew 5:9 (MSG) encourages, "You're blessed when you can show people how to cooperate instead of compete or fight. That's when you discover who you really are, and your place in God's family." Democracy is based on the notion that "none of us is as smart as all of us." Competition has its role in our society, but the individual who values teamwork is one who moves society forward.

Democracy is based on the notion that "none of us is as smart as all of us." Competition has its role in our society, but the individual who values teamwork is one who moves society forward.

Learning to cooperate begins in the family and the classroom. It is fostered through everyday problem solving and planning, which require effective communication and a spirit of mutual respect and participation. In Chapter 2 we will present communication skills that will help you cultivate the cooperation of your children while teaching them to solve problems and make decisions cooperatively with others. And in every chapter, we will present a Family Enrichment Activity to help you strengthen the relationship between you and your child.

Respect

The concept of mutual respect is a cornerstone of life in any democratic society, particularly one that includes a lot of diversity. Treating others respectfully and expecting them to treat you the same, allows for the free sharing of ideas that eventually solve problems and create a better society for everyone. On the other hand, lack of respect in a democratic society creates an atmosphere of resentment and hostility that leads to conflict and even aggression.

Teaching our children to respect us is only the beginning. Teaching them to respect God, themselves, others, and their environment is what will really make a difference. In Psalm 33:18-19 (MSG), we are told: "God's eye is on those who respect him, the ones who are looking for his love. He's ready to come to their rescue in bad times; in lean times he keeps body and soul together." We are blessed to bless our children and their joy, character, and living faith will bless the world around them. May the following verse from Deuteronomy 28:10 (MSG) be true of every member of our family: "All the peoples on Earth will see you living under the Name of God and hold you in respectful awe."

Self-Esteem

Self-esteem is born out of the blessing of Ephesians 3:16-17 (NLT): "I pray that from (God's) glorious, unlimited resources he will empower you with inner strength through his Spirit. Then Christ will make his home in your hearts as you trust in him. Your roots will grow down into God's love and keep you strong."

Children who believe they are worthwhile human beings with God-given talents and dreams that are worthy of respect, have the best chance of thriving. In fact, high self-esteem helps a person develop the other character traits that are needed to succeed: courage, responsibility, and cooperation. At the same time, seeing oneself as someone who embodies these positive qualities, with faith as the solid foundation, builds higher self-esteem. We will explore this cycle further in Chapter 4, as we look at how to help children build self-esteem based on character and actions, not self-hype.

Of course, you will want to encourage your children to develop additional qualities of character besides these essential six. The skills you learn here will encourage the development of the Christian values that are important in your family. These same skills will also work to reduce the conflicts and hassles of everyday living and make your home a more joyful place for everyone to thrive.

Styles of Parenting

Our goal as parents, then, is to instill in our children the skills and character that will enable them to survive and thrive at home, in school, in the faith community, and eventually as independent adults in our fast-changing, diverse, democratic society. This is our responsibility, and we have the authority to get the job done. After all, even in a society of equals, authorities still exist. The president of a corporation, the police officer on the street, and the principal of a school are examples of people who have the authority to make final decisions — and the responsibility to enforce those decisions. They are the leaders. However, there's not much use being a leader if no one is willing to follow you. Here is an important principle of leadership:

Leaders get their ultimate authority from those they lead.

The same is true for parents. We are the authorities in our families. But to be effective, we must have the cooperation of our children. How you choose to guide your child in the development of character, skills, and behavior is a matter of personal preference. No two parents are exactly alike, so no two parents will parent exactly alike. However, if we eliminate parents at the extremes — those who are abusive or neglectful — the rest tend towards one of three major styles of parenting: an autocratic style (the "Dictator"); a permissive style ("the Doormat"); or an authoritative style ("the Active Parent").

The reason we said "tend towards" is that most parents actually exhibit characteristics of all three parenting styles at different times, depending on their child's behavior, their mood, and other factors. This inconsistency encourages children to test their parents to see how far they can push the limits. By understanding the three styles and knowing which one you tend towards, you'll have a better chance of applying the Active style of parenting with greater consistency.[2]

1. The Autocratic Style: The Dictator

The autocratic parent tries to be all-powerful in directing the lives of his children. This parent is usually a dominating, authoritarian figure — a Dictator — that uses reward and punishment as tools to enforce his orders. Kids are kept in line by the threat of punishment if they misbehave and the promise of reward if they do what they are told. Kids are told what to do, how to do it, and when and where to do it. There is little or no room for them to question, challenge, or

Even in a society of equals, authorities still exist: people who have the authority to make final decisions—and the responsibility to enforce those decisions.

---

[2] If you would like some help in determining your parenting style, there is a free quiz you can take on our website at http://www.activeparenting.com/Parents-Parenting_Style_Quiz that can give you some insight.

disagree. Sometimes autocratic parents take a more subtle approach, using a combination of guilt, disapproval, and other emotional tactics to keep their kids in line. The common factor in all autocratic parents is a desire to control.

Children brought up in autocratic families seldom thrive. Sometimes their spirits are broken and they give up. More often, they rebel. This rebellion can be characterized by sneaking or by open defiance. Rebellion usually happens during the teen years, because by then the child has developed enough power — both physical and intellectual — to fight back. Autocratic parenting has been the typical parenting style for so many generations that teenage rebellion has come to be accepted by many experts as "normal." This is a mistake. Kids raised with an Active style of parenting do not have to rebel to become independent.

The autocratic style of parenting can be described as "limits without freedom," which we can show as a closed circle.

Autocratic Style (The Dictator)

Limits without Freedom

This parenting method worked reasonably well when inequality was the norm in our society and the culture dictated that "children should be seen but not heard"; however, it works poorly in today's world of increased equality.

The autocratic parent deserves some credit for recognizing the need for limits and having the emotional strength to stand firm. But this parent goes much too far.

You are tending toward the autocratic style of parenting if you say things like:

■ "Because I'm the parent and I said so!"

■ "As long as you live under my roof, you'll obey my rules."

■ "When you are the parent, you can decide what to do."

And when you do things like:

■ tell your child what to wear.

■ find yourself angry and yelling frequently.

■ ground or punish your child in other ways.

The autocratic parent deserves some credit for recognizing the need for limits and having the emotional strength to stand firm. But this parent goes much too far.

2. The Permissive Style: The Doormat

Permissive parents are often those who react strongly against the harsh and uncompromising autocratic method. Instead, they allow their children too much freedom. In such households, there is little respect for order and routine, and few limits are placed on anyone's freedom. Children often have no curfew and few household responsibilities. They are pampered and, as a result, become accustomed to getting their own way. Permissive parents tend to behave like doormats, allowing their children to walk all over them.

Kids who grow up with this style of parenting may act like they enjoy the excessive freedom they are allowed, but without a clear authority figure to protect and guide them, underneath they feel insecure. Privately, they may even wish to have limits imposed on them. As one older child wrote in her blog, "I need rules. I need to hear someone say "no." I need a mom, not another friend." Children with permissive parents sometimes lack a sense of belonging with the family, and because they have not learned to cooperate, they may be difficult to live with. They often rebel against authority or refuse to comply with rules. These unfortunate effects often follow them into adulthood, where, accustomed to a lifestyle with no limits, they may have trouble keeping a job and struggle with the healthy give and take of close relationships.

The permissive method can be described as "freedom without limits" and shown as a zigzag line, meaning freedom run rampant.

Permissive Style (The Doormat)

Freedom without Limits

Although it is commendable that permissive parents understand the need for freedom and are willing to share power with their children, they go too far also.

Although it is commendable that permissive parents understand the need for freedom and are willing to share power with their children, they go too far also.

You are tending toward the permissive parenting style when you say things like:

- "I don't think that's a good idea … but, well … OK, if you really want to."

- "Do you really need this? Oh, all right. Here's the money."

- "I sure wish you'd pick up after yourself."

And when you do things like:

- ignore your child's schoolwork until you see his low grades.

- act as your child's alarm clock and wake-up service.

- give in to her unreasonable demands because you're afraid she will become angry or sad.

3. The Authoritative Style: The Active Parent

The Active Parenting style is in some respects the middle ground between the autocratic method and permissive method. It is also much more. In an Active household, freedom is important, but so are the rights of others and the responsibilities of all. The parent is a leader who encourages order and routine and understands the need for reasonable limits to behavior. The Active Parenting method acknowledges a system of modern social equality in which every member of the family is important and worthy of respect.

Active Parenting acknowledges our democratic heritage and the role of social equality among all human beings.

Active Parenting acknowledges our democratic heritage and the role of social equality among all human beings in two important ways:

- Parents treat children with dignity and respect, even during discipline.

- Children are entitled to respectfully express their thoughts and feelings to their parents. In this way they are given the right to influence the decisions that affect their lives.

This is consistent with life in a democratic society:

*Democracy does not mean that
you will always get your way;
it means you will always get your say.*

It is also consistent with Christian belief and values:

"You are free to eat from any tree in the garden; but you must not eat from the tree of the knowledge of good and evil."

Genesis 2:16-17a (NIV)

From the beginning of creation, God blessed human beings with three powerful words: "You are free." Yet God also gave us clear limits: "...but you must not eat from the tree of the knowledge of good and evil." This is a method we call "freedom with limits." It is a central tenet of the Active style of parenting and is at the very root of Christian living. It can be shown as a zigzag line within the limits of a circle.

Authoritative Style (The Active Parent)

Freedom within Limits

It would also be appropriate to call the Active style "freedom within expanding limits," because as the child grows up and assumes more responsibility, the Active Parent gradually relaxes limits until eventually, as an 18-21 year old, their child has the same amount of independence as any adult. This is what expanding limits means.

Freedom within Expanding Limits

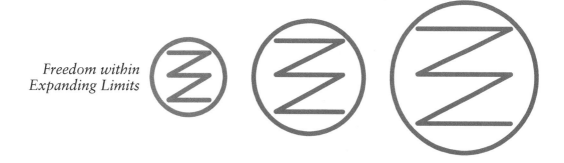

"You are called to freedom, brothers and sisters; only don't let this freedom be an opportunity to indulge your selfish impulses, but serve each other through love."

Galatians 5:13 (CEB)

We have a duty to use God's gift of freedom responsibly, staying within the limits of the law in our society and the Christian faith. In this way we provide an example for our children to follow as they test their own freedom.

You are tending toward the Active style of parenting when you say things like:

- "I know you're disappointed, but you can't go. Here's why…"

- "Sure we can talk about it. What's your idea?"

- "I know you can handle it. But if you need some help, just let me know."

And when you do things like:

- involve your child in deciding who will do which family chores.

- give her responsibility over her homework, monitoring her only as needed.

- show an active interest in his education by asking what he is learning in school, Sunday School, Youth Group, and church.

- talk with her about your expectations for her behavior and the consequences for breaking agreements.

- talk with him about topics such as drug use, sexuality, and violence in a calm and non-judgmental manner.

- let her know what you like about her and encourage her often.

The Parenting Style Continuum

In this book we present the Active style of parenting as the most effective of the three styles, as well as the most compatible with our modern democratic society and Christian faith. That does not mean Dictator- and Doormat-style parents are entirely wrong in their approaches. In fact, both of these styles have their strengths.

Comparing the Styles of Parenting

	Dictator ◯	**Doormat** ⋜	**Active** ⓩ
Weaknesses	Reactive Out of sync with life in a democracy Invites rebellion or crushes spirit Low in support	Inactive/Reactive Out of sync with life in a democracy Fails to teach or spoils Low in discipline	
Strengths	Setting Limits Firmness (discipline) Parent is confident	Providing choices Nurturing (support) Parent is caring	Pro-active Combines discipline and support Firm and nurturing Confident and caring Invites cooperation

Imagine the three parenting styles on a continuum:

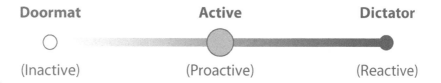

Doormat	Active	Dictator
◯	⬤	⬤
(Inactive)	(Proactive)	(Reactive)

The Active style, with its proactive approach balanced between the extremes of inactive (Doormat) and reactive (Dictator) parenting, in many ways combines the best of both styles. An Active Parent is both flexible and firm, allowing the child freedom … within limits. As you progress through this guide and practice the skills you learn, you will move toward a balanced, proactive center as an Active Parent.

Be honest about the way you were parented and what parenting style you have implemented up until now. As mentioned before, in our homes we often repeat the way we were parented or we go to the opposite extreme, parenting in reaction to the way we were raised. Admitting that some of your old parenting habits were detrimental allows you to shed those behaviors, making room for a new set of skills. Permissive parents can become Active Parents. Reactive parents can become Active Parents. This transformation requires a desire to improve as a parent — an openness to the value of the Christian Active Parenting approach, and the courage to tap into the Holy Spirit's power.

A Little Bit about Your Child's Brain

A strong case can be made that the human brain was God's most complex living creation. Although there is still much about this amazing organ that we do not understand, scientists have learned a great deal during the past ten years alone. A helpful approach to understanding the human brain is to think of it as comprised of three major parts.

The most basic part of the brain, sometimes called the "Old Brain" because it is a part that we have in common with many lesser developed animals, consists of a brain stem and a cerebellum. These control basic survival needs, like breathing, swallowing, physical coordination, and other basic instincts. One of these instincts is called the "fight or flight" response to danger, which means that when we feel threatened, we are wired to either fight or run. Being instinctual, this decision does not require any thinking. That's good if the goal is

2
Emotional Brain
- Emotions
- Memory
- Bonding

3
Rational Brain
- "Executive Center"
- Still under construction in children

1
Old Brain
- Basic Survival Functions
- Instinctual behavior
- "Fight or flight" response

simply to survive, but if the goal is to thrive in a modern society, this instinct can cause problems. So while the primitive Old Brain enabled our ancestors to survive, it didn't do so well in helping them thrive.

A second and more complex part of the brain is called the "Emotional Brain" because it controls such things as motivation and emotion. It enables humans to feel things like fear, joy, anger, caring, separation distress, playfulness, and love. This is a great advantage for humans in many ways, but emotions require management. Fortunately, humans also have a third part of the brain, which forms around the first two. This is the "Rational Brain," otherwise known as the cerebral cortex, and it is what most separates humankind from all other species on Earth. At the front of this part of the brain is the prefrontal cortex, which is considered the "executive center" of the brain because it controls higher human functions like:

- Sound decision-making
- Empathy
- Consideration of consequences
- Regulation of emotions
- Self-awareness
- Morality

At birth, a baby's brain is like the Old Brain, with its brainstem and cerebellum being the only parts that are anywhere near fully developed. It is focused mainly on survival. But brains develop fast, and around a child's first birthday, the Emotional Brain is starting to allow them more complex responses. Around age seven, the rational part of the brain picks up developmental speed. It then hits a huge growth spurt between ages 12 and 14—the onset of puberty, and continues developing until age 25 to 30.

You may have noticed that brain growth occurs from the back of the brain to the front. This explains why children and teens still need the help of parents and other adults for guidance. Although they are learning fast, they just do not have the brain development yet to operate independently, at least not as well as they will later.

When we push kids too hard, expect too much too soon, or otherwise put them under too much stress, the Old Brain releases a chemical called *cortisol*. It's part of that "fight or flight" response in humans. The resulting anger, tantrums, or shutting down is a normal part of a child's development. But if this chemical is released too often or for too long, as can happen with kids who experience a lot of stress (for example, ongoing abuse or neglect), the prolonged presence of cortisol in the body can actually slow down normal brain development and hinder the child's ability to handle stress in the future.

Fortunately, there are other chemicals called *opioids* (for example, oxytocin) that provide children with feelings of comfort and well-being and enable them to thrive. Children's brains produce these chemicals when their parents hold them, hug them, or show them care and affection. In other words, when children "feel felt" by their parents and other care givers.

Parents who tend towards the Dictator or Doormat styles of parenting put their children under too much stress, causing the release of cortisol and blocking the release of opioids. Active Parents provide or allow their children to experience appropriate stress, are able to

CAP methods will help you promote healthy growth and development of your child's brain to help them survive and thrive at home, at school, and beyond.

calm and comfort their children when needed, and provide physical affection, all of which causes the release of oxytocin and other opioids, which promote bonding and thriving.

The CAP methods you will be learning will help you promote the healthy growth and development of your child's brain to help them survive and thrive at home, at school, and beyond.

We'll be focusing on three specific skill areas throughout this program:

- Nurturing and support skills: How you build a strong relationship with your children, teach them how to better relate to others, and nurture your and your children's relationships with God

- Discipline skills: How you help your children learn from the consequences of their actions

- Problem-solving skills: How you help your children learn to cope with conflict and make difficult decisions

Practicing these skills on a daily basis will not only improve your relationship with your children; it will also work invisibly in their developing brains, strengthening connections in the prefrontal cortex in ways that will last a lifetime.

Why Strong Leaders Build Strong Relationships

Many parents buy a parenting book or take a parenting course in hopes of finding the magic bullet of discipline. It doesn't exist. There are certainly tricks you can use to modify your child's behavior and bend him to your will, but these methods usually fall short in the long run. What works much better for most leaders is a combination of solid discipline skills and a strong, loving relationship. The core of Christianity is based on a relationship with God rather than religion. God wants a loving relationship with us, not merely to have us follow a list of rules out of fear. A strong, loving relationship increases your

A strong, loving relationship increases your ability to influence your child. Your ideas will matter more to him. So will your approval or disapproval, your rules, and your discipline.

ability to influence your child. Your ideas will matter more to him. So will your approval or disapproval, your rules and your discipline. Build a strong relationship and your child (or anyone you want to lead) will more likely come around to your way of thinking about most things — not all things, because that would be counterproductive. After all, progress is only made when one generation improves upon the previous generation. You will be learning many skills to help build your relationship with your child or others, including:

- mutual respect
- participation
- problem solving
- family enrichment
- communication
- encouragement

We will take a look at the first two of these in this chapter and the others later.

Mutual Respect

Our children are growing up in a society in which people are very sensitive to signs of disrespect. To disrespect somebody is often considered a personal affront — one that can even lead to violence. It is no wonder that successful leaders have learned that treating others respectfully is essential to long-term success.

The author Bernard Malamud once wrote, "Respect is something you have to give in order to get."

Likewise, learning to respect oneself regardless of strengths, weaknesses, family, culture, or heritage is a building block for self-esteem and success. When you show your child respect, even when you are angry or providing discipline, you help her learn to respect herself while demonstrating how to treat others respectfully.

In fact, treating your child respectfully demonstrates how they should treat *you* respectfully. As the author Bernard Malamud once wrote, "Respect is something you have to give in order to get." In other words, if we want someone to treat us respectfully, our children

included, then we have to be willing to treat them respectfully, too. This concept of "mutual respect," as Rudolf Dreikurs called it, is often easier said than done. Showing children respect means not yelling, cursing, calling them names, being sarcastic, or otherwise speaking to them in ways you would not want them speaking to you. There are also countless more subtle forms of disrespect to guard against. For example, when an overprotective dad is quick to jump in to solve his daughter's problem without giving her a chance to struggle to find a solution for herself, he is being disrespectful. A mom who always insists on doing what she wants and never compromising to do what her son wants is also showing disrespect.

When you catch yourself treating your child disrespectfully, it is wise to smile, apologize, and if appropriate, make amends. For example:

> *"Please forgive me for yelling at you. That wasn't very respectful. Let me try again more calmly to tell you why I was angry."*

> *"I apologize for not calling to say I'd be late. How can I make it up to you?"*

As you make this effort to treat your child respectfully, insist that your child show you respect as well. This will probably require teaching on your part, since children do not always know how to be respectful, so help them along. For example:

> *"I don't talk to you that way. Please do not talk to me that way."*

> *"I don't talk to you that way. I won't tolerate you talking to me that way."*

> *"I want the two of you to stop right now. We don't talk to each other that way in our family. It is disrespectful."*

As we will see in Chapter 3, when your words alone are not enough to correct misbehavior, respectful discipline is called for. One effective method is to use a logically connected consequence to help get your message through. For example:

"Either talk to me without yelling or go to your room."

"Either share the remote without fighting or there will be no TV for either of you."

"Either talk to me respectfully about not letting you watch inappropriate movies or there will be no movies at all this week."

When mutual respect is a cornerstone of your own interactions with people, your children come to adopt it almost without trying.

The respect with which you treat your spouse or significant other, your extended family, your friends, and even strangers also sets an example for your child. When mutual respect is a cornerstone of your own interactions with people, your children come to adopt it almost without trying.

The Method of Choice

Human choice is one of the most powerful forces in existence. This concept is so powerful that nations go to war to preserve their right to choose how to live their lives. When we say that the hallmark of the Active style of parenting is "freedom within limits," what we are really talking about is the freedom of the child to make choices.

Just as a people will rise up and overthrow a dictator, a child will resist a parent who robs her of a chance to share in the decisions that affect her life. The parent who is neither a Dictator nor a Doormat, but an Active Christian leader in the family, will use this knowledge to handle problems and teach responsibility.

Choice is power. But making *good* choices is a skill, one that requires experience. You can give your child this experience by offering choices that are appropriate for his age and level of responsibility. This, again, is the idea of freedom within *expanding* limits. The freedom to choose is tremendously empowering to children. And because you exercise your authority to limit what choices the child is allowed to make, family rules and Christian values are not sacrificed.

> *Choice is power. But making good choices is a skill, one that requires experience.*

Don't Boss. Give a Choice.

Even young children can be given simple choices. Allowing your child the opportunity to practice decision-making can become a regular part of your daily routine. This can also be useful in helping resolve conflicts. For example, after unsuccessfully trying to coerce her son into drinking his orange juice, Laura gives her son, Nicholas, a choice.

> Laura: *Would you rather have orange juice this morning or apple juice?*
>
> Nicholas: *Apple juice!*

This gives Nicholas some power over the decisions that affect his life, so he has less need to rebel. He chooses apple juice, which is acceptable to Laura. Had he chosen a juice that wasn't available, Laura would have limited his choice.

> Laura: *I'm sorry, Nicholas, we don't have grape juice, but I'll be glad to pick some up the next time I go shopping. Would you like that?*
>
> Nicholas: *Yes.*
>
> Laura: *Great. I'll put it on my shopping list. Now, what's it going to be for today, apple or orange?*

As children get older, parents can start giving them more open-ended choices. So instead of asking Nicholas to choose either apple or orange juice, Laura might simply ask him what he would like to drink. The following are some examples of appropriate choices for children of different age ranges:

Choices for Children Ages 4-7 :

"Would you like to brush your teeth before you wash your face or after?"

"Can you put this away yourself, or would you like some help?"

"Would you like to pick out a book or would you like me to choose one for your bedtime story?"

"Would you like to take your bath now or after one more song?"

Choices for Children Ages 8-12:

"Would you like to help me do the grocery shopping and help choose what we buy?"

"Do you prefer to set homework time for before dinner or afterwards?"

"Would you rather go visit Grandma on Saturday or Sunday after church?"

"Which chores would you like to do?"

A word of caution: Don't get carried away and make *everything* a choice. Sometimes children want and need a firm but friendly decision from a parent. At other times, a limited set of choices is appreciated.

You and Your Partner: Agreement of Support

If you are a parent in a committed relationship, you may sometimes wonder what to do if you and your partner have different parenting styles. Of course, it's best if you both adopt an Active style of parenting, but when that is not possible, focus on your own relationship with your children. Rather than using your new knowledge of Christian Active Parenting skills to criticize or berate your partner, work towards supporting each other in spite of your differences. Also, avoid saying things to your children that will undermine the other parent. Go over the following agreement with your partner and use it as a basis for putting your children first.

WE AGREE TO...

- put the best interests of our children ahead of our differences.

- respect each other's right to see our children's needs differently.

- discuss our differences in private, not in front of our children.

- be open to new ways of parenting.

- agree on how to handle situations together, compromising rather than bullying each other or giving in.

- present a united front to our children, so that they are not tempted to pit us against one another.

- avoid undermining each other by criticizing the other parent to the children, changing agreements without consulting each other, or otherwise trying to "score points" with our children at the expense of the other.

- look for the positive in each other's parenting methods and encourage each other by pointing these positives out.

- seek God's perspective on conflicts through prayer and open discussion with each other.

Family Enrichment Activity: Taking Time for Fun

Ever notice that a good salesperson will always spend time developing a positive relationship with you before she tries to sell you anything? She knows that half the job of effectively influencing someone is first developing a relationship. Once the person has been "won over," the sale is much easier to make. (Can you imagine a salesperson being autocratic and demanding a sale? "You'll buy this because I'm the salesperson and I said so!")

The same is true for parenting. The more you can enrich your relationship with your child, the more of an influence you will have in his life. This will prevent many problems, as well as make discipline much easier when it is called for.

The key is to have fun and to try making it a regular part of your relationship. In other words, "Every day a little play."

At the end of each chapter, we will present a family enrichment activity. If you and your child frequently have power struggles, these weekly activities designed to strengthen relationships can help you begin making positive contact. Be creative. Reach out. Have fun together.

In fact, our first family enrichment activity is to take time to do something fun with your child. It can be as brief as a few minutes or as long as a day. The key is to have fun and to try making it a regular part of your relationship. In other words, "Every day a little play." For example:

- Throw a ball or shoot baskets
- Bake a special dessert together
- Play a game together
- Roughhouse
- Go on an outing...just the two of you
- Go for a walk or take a hike
- Tickle each other
- Tell a joke or a funny story

■ Have a sing-along in the car (Sources of fun and wholesome songs include Sunday school, camp, youth group, and Christian radio.)

To get the most out of this activity:

■ Find activities you both enjoy; many have little or no cost.

■ Ask for suggestions from your child, but have some ideas of your own.

■ Keep it fun! Do not use this time for confrontation.

■ Record your experiences by writing about them or taking pictures or videos.

Get active. Get your kids active.

According to the Centers for Disease Control (CDC), child obesity has more than doubled in children and tripled in adolescents in the past 30 years. More than one third of children were found to be overweight or obese. Not only is this unhealthy, but it also means that kids (and parents) are missing out on the other benefits that physical activity bring to the human brain and body. After all, we evolved to be active participants on this beautiful planet, not passive watchers. The National Institutes of Health recommends that children get at least an hour of physical activity every day. Regular exercise helps them:

■ Feel less stressed

■ Feel better about themselves

■ Feel more ready to learn in school

■ Keep a healthy weight

■ Build and keep healthy bones, muscles, and joints

■ Sleep better at night

Here are some ideas for promoting healthy habits in your family:

■ Make time for the entire family to participate in regular physical activities like walking, biking, or rollerblading.

■ Assign active chores such as vacuuming, washing the car, or mowing the lawn to each family member.

■ Encourage your child to join a sports team at school or a recreation center.

■ Limit the amount of screen time your child engages in (that includes TV, video, and computer time).

■ Serve a healthy diet, limiting fried foods, sugar, and other unhealthy products.

■ Encourage your children to be part of the planning, preparation, and cooking of some of their meals.

■ Eat more meals together at the dinner table at regular times.

■ Have healthy snack food available, such as fruit, vegetables, and yogurt.

■ Avoid serving portions that are too large. When you eat out at restaurants, share large portions.

■ Avoid using food as a reward or withholding food as a punishment.

■ Avoid forcing your child to eat when he/she is not hungry. (If your child is losing too much weight, consult a healthcare professional.)

■ Limit fast food consumption to no more than once a week (and don't "supersize" it).

Family Meeting: Choosing a Family Activity

The Christian Active Parenting model is designed to teach your child the skills and traits needed to survive and thrive in a democratic society, where everyone may not get their way, but they always get their say. By holding family meetings, you can provide an opportunity for your children to participate and make choices that help guide the family. This will help your family run more smoothly while teaching your kids the give and take that comes with cooperative problem solving and decision making. That is why we will present a family meeting at the end of each chapter.

This week's family meeting is to decide what fun activity your family will choose for one of your "Taking Time for Fun" family enrichment activities this week. Use the following tips to help hold a successful family meeting.

Tips for Holding Family Meetings

Parents are usually the ones to present the idea of holding a family meeting and get the meetings started. Here are some points for you to consider in setting up a family meeting.

Who Should Attend Family Meetings?

Family meetings should include parents, children, and anyone else who lives with the family, such as grandparents, uncles, or aunts. In other words, you should invite anyone who has a stake in decisions affecting the daily life of the family.

But don't make attendance mandatory. Start with those who are willing to attend. Some family members may not be ready for a whole-family discussion, or they might feel the idea of holding family meetings is not a good one. But this doesn't mean the family should abandon the idea. If most family members want to hold meetings, go ahead with the plan. Those who do not attend the early meetings may decide to attend later when they see the advantages.

Single-Parent Households

Families affected by separation or divorce can still hold family meetings, even though one parent will not be participating. In those cases it is important for the family to avoid discussing matters pertaining to the children's relationship with the absent parent. Those matters are between the children and the absent parent and should be handled by Active Communication.

Time and Place

Select a time and a place convenient and agreeable to everyone who will be attending. A good time for family meetings is Sunday afternoons, since that is the beginning of the week and the family is more likely to be together at that time. The meetings should be held in a place comfortable for all participants, preferably around a table with enough room for everyone to pull up a chair.

Keep the meeting informal and brief. This will help ensure that nobody comes to resent the forum.

Ground Rules

At your first family meeting, it's important to agree on the ground rules everyone will follow during the meeting. Start by suggesting and getting agreement on one basic ground rule. For example:

We will treat each other respectfully.

Next, ask everyone to contribute some ideas about what that means to them. For example:

We will begin and end our meeting with prayer.

We will listen while someone else is speaking.

We will wait until the speaker is finished before speaking.

We will not insult or put down anybody else's ideas.

Write down everyone's ideas and develop a master list of family meeting ground rules. Here's an example:

Family Meeting Ground Rules

DO:

- Begin and end with prayer.
- Listen when others are speaking.
- Speak respectfully.
- Invite everyone's ideas.
- Share how you think and feel.
- Encourage others.

DON'T:

- Put anyone's ideas down.
- Interrupt.
- Monopolize the discussion.
- Consider only your own point of view.
- Criticize others.
- Call anyone names.

Once you establish ground rules for your family meetings, it will be easier to run the meetings smoothly and keep everyone in a positive frame of mind. If a family member violates one of these rules in a meeting, simply remind him with a firm, calm comment such as, "Didn't we agree that we wouldn't criticize each other?"

Be careful, however, not to turn the meeting into a confrontation. Your goal is to establish family meetings as enjoyable times that allow children to have their voices heard and their wishes considered. Stay upbeat and encouraging as much as possible and you will find that family meetings are a great benefit to parents and children alike.

Your goal is to establish family meetings as enjoyable times that allow children to have their voices heard and their wishes considered.

Taking Care of the Caregiver

We began this chapter by saying that parenting is a very active undertaking and that it requires a lot of energy to do well. You might think of this energy as a pitcher of water which you pour out of all day as you take care of the needs of your family, career, volunteer activities, friends, and other demands. By the end of the day, this energy can be used up, and your pitcher completely empty.

The idea of taking care of the caregiver (namely you) is that you have to take time each day to restore yourself. While some parents think that taking personal time is selfish, the truth is that you can't do your best if you are constantly overwhelmed, exhausted, burned out, or just plain irritable. Of course, there are parents who go to an extreme in taking care of themselves to the detriment of their children and significant others.

While some parents think that taking personal time is selfish, the truth is that you can't do your best if you are constantly overwhelmed, exhausted, burned out, or just plain irritable.

Self-care means to systematically plan (and take!) time away from your children to care for yourself and your other relationships. The following areas can help you plan:

Strengthen your mind through Bible study. Jesus was a well-versed student of the ancient holy texts. He knew how to walk in the ways of God because he studied those ways diligently. As parents, we also benefit from being well-versed students of the Bible. Joining a small group Bible study or taking time to study Scripture can give us the guidance we need to shepherd our children in the ways of the Lord. Flawed biblical characters are people just like us. They deal with favoritism in families and sibling rivalry, disobedient kids and disloyal family members, a human tendency to stray from God and the challenge of passing along faith to uninterested children. Dive into Scripture and see how the Lord has actively parented humankind in the ways of faith, generation after generation.

Keep your body healthy. When you are a parent, your body is your instrument. You touch and hug your children, lift them up and hold their hands, walk alongside them and play with them. You want to be healthy and active for years to come. Everyone in your family will benefit from you taking care of your physical body. Refer to the list in the section, "Get Active. Get Your Kids Active." As the caregiver for yourself and your family, you will do well to adopt the same healthy habits you are promoting in your children.

Surround yourself with a godly support system. Jesus spent quality time with his best friends. Yes, He was constantly approached by a multitude of needy people, but He regularly retreated to connect with His closest companions. Even though the demands on His time were great, Jesus valued time with His disciples as a top priority. He shared meals with them often; He walked, talked, and ministered with them regularly; and He and His best friends learned God's lessons together. We care for ourselves as caregivers when we make time for friends and family members who build us up and give us support. The church is a great place to find these connections. Join a Sunday school class, sing in the choir, volunteer to be a greeter, host a Bible study in your home, become a member of a Christian parenting group. There are no limits to the creative ways we can build Christian community.

We care for ourselves as caregivers when we make time for friends and family members who build us up and give us support.

Get organized. A lack of structure and organization is bad for kids and parents alike. When you are constantly worrying about things falling through the cracks and not getting done, you are expending needless energy. Simple time management tools include making and using "to do" lists each day, keeping a family calendar of everyone's activities, and taking time to organize each part of your home. Prayerfully discerning God's priorities for your time as a family will allow you to accomplish the Lord's "to do" list each day. Prune from your schedule those commitments that hinder your growth as a family of faith.

Decide how you want to handle romance. We are not only spiritual and intellectual, emotional and relational beings; we are also sexual beings. Not everyone has the same goals about romance in their lives.

Some single parents are content to spend time with adult friends and their children, perhaps putting off romance until the kids are grown. Others actively date with or without the intention of marriage. Take some time to think about what is best for you and your family and then actively pursue it. Just be sure that you balance everyone's needs. If you are married or in a significant relationship, it is important to take care of your couple relationship. This means going out without the kids at times and taking adult-only vacations. You'd be surprised how the romance can re-bloom when you have a little privacy someplace away from home. And if your marriage needs the help of a counselor, check with your local mental health center, a physician, or other resource for a good referral.

Clear your mind. Generals talk about something called the "haze of battle." Surrounded by noise and commotion, soldiers in combat sometimes lose track of what is really going on. That is when they are most likely to make errors in judgment. Now consider the "haze of parenthood." In the near-chaos of daily life with children, parents can lose their sense of the big picture. When you feel on the verge of becoming overwhelmed, take a little time out to clear your mind. Lying down on your bed for 10 minutes with the door closed can do wonders. Other methods include spending time outdoors, listening to music, or reading. And a critical way of clearing your mind is to maintain the most important relationship in the world, your intimate relationship with God.

Quiet Time with God

> "Blessed are those who have learned to acclaim you,
> who walk in the light of your presence, Lord."
>
> *Psalm 89:15 (NIV)*

We are told in Luke 5:16 (CEV) that "Jesus would often go to some place where he could be alone and pray." Whenever He was making a difficult decision or facing a challenge, He got away to a quiet place, laid down His burdens, and prayed for as long as He needed. This equipped Him to make healthy, loving decisions, day after day. Following in Jesus's footsteps as Christian parents, we need to spend time regularly with God in order to make the healthy, loving decisions that our family requires, day after day.

When we take time away from our family to be with God alone, we get beneath our worries, our fears, and other feelings that overwhelm us to enjoy the peaceful presence of the Holy Spirit.

When we take time away from our family to be with God alone, we get beneath our worries, our fears, and other feelings that overwhelm us to enjoy the peaceful presence of the Holy Spirit. 1 Corinthians 6:19 (AMP) asks an important question: "Do you not know that your body is the temple (the very sanctuary) of the Holy Spirit Who lives within you, Whom you have received (as a Gift) from God?" We can visit this inner sanctuary any time of day or night. God will shed new light on our parenting challenges and we will arise from our quiet time filled with fresh insight, equipped to actively share the love of God in our homes.

God is also our best source of stress release. The Lord says in Matthew 11:28 (NIV), "Come to me, all you who are weary and burdened, and I will give you rest." Similarly, 1 Peter 5:7 (NLT) encourages: "Give all your worries and cares to God, for he cares about you." A strong personal prayer life allows us to release our cares to God, giving ourselves rest from our weary burdens.

What forms of prayer work best for you? Lighting a candle to focus your quiet time? Journaling your honest feelings to God? An energizing study of Scripture? Escaping into nature? A long, hot bath? Writing, singing, or creating something? Sweating out stress through your favorite exercise? Meditation, guided imagery, or yoga? Praying aloud or silently? Whatever your best forms of prayer, make sure to lay down the burdens of your heart often. Empty yourself before God and rest in His presence, and be filled up with the power of the Holy Spirit.

Sometimes, we don't know how to pray or what to say to God, "And the Holy Spirit helps us in our weakness. For example, we don't know what God wants us to pray for ... And the Father who knows all hearts knows what the Spirit is saying, for the Spirit pleads for us believers in harmony with God's own will" (Romans 8:26-27, NLT). When you cannot put words to the turmoil in your heart, trust the Holy Spirit to speak for you. Through prayer, we exchange our problems for God's peace.

> **"If you would have a peaceful heart and strength to meet the day;
> Spend some time alone with God to read His word and pray."**
>
> *Author Unknown*

Remember to Practice!

Learning new skills — from riding a bike to using a computer program to learning new parenting techniques — requires practice. And the more you practice, the better the results. As you read each chapter and learn powerful parenting skills and techniques, it's very important that you take time to put these ideas to work in your family. We recommend that you read one chapter and then, before moving on to the next, give yourself a full week to practice your new skills with your family. Record your experiences on the worksheets found in the companion Workbook or in a journal of your own making.

Even with practice, it's important that you do not expect your kids to change this week.

Even with practice, it's important that you do not expect your kids to change this week. It is sometimes easy to forget that it took years to develop some of the problems that you may experience with your child. Just as it takes a large ship time to change its course after the rudders are adjusted, it will take time before you begin to see positive changes in the course of your relationship with your child. As you become more familiar with the skills you are learning, these techniques will become more and more natural to you, and you'll begin to see positive changes.

We leave you with a blessing as we begin this Christian Active Parenting adventure together:

> **"May the God of hope**
> **fill you with all joy and peace**
> **as you trust in him,**
> **so that you may overflow with hope**
> **by the power of the Holy Spirit."**
>
> *Romans 15:13 (NIV)*

May you experience joy with your family this week and feel a growing sense of hope and peace as you move forward to become the best parent you can be.

CHAPTER 2: Cooperation & Communication

> *An oarsman in a Roman galley was rowing to the beat of the drum. He looked over at the oarsman next to him and was horrified at what he saw. The oarsman in the next seat was drilling a hole in the bottom of the boat under his seat. As the water began to gush into the boat, the first oarsman exclaimed, "What in Jupiter's name are you doing?" The other man replied, "What's it to you? I'm only drilling the hole under my seat."*

T he point of this story, of course, is that when we are all riding in the same boat, no matter whose seat the hole is under, everyone is going to get wet. Nowhere is this truer than in a family. When one member has a problem, the ripples are felt throughout the family.

A child who learns to work cooperatively with others has a far greater chance of success than a child who stands alone.

Remember the six main qualities of character that form the foundation of the individual's ability to succeed in our democratic society? They are: faith, courage, self-esteem, responsibility, respect, and cooperation. Cooperation, the gentle art of working together for the common good, is the subject of this chapter. Let's begin with a definition:

cooperation:

Two or more people working together in a mutually supportive manner toward a common goal

The reason democratic societies flourish while those based on dictatorship or lawlessness flounder is in large measure due to the fact that *none of us is as smart as all of us.* When people work together cooperatively, problems are solved and civilizations are built. Likewise, a child who learns to work cooperatively with others has a far greater chance of success than a child who stands alone or one who is in constant conflict. Most parents *say* that they want cooperation, but ...

Dictators DEMAND cooperation.

Doormats HOPE for cooperation.

Christian Active Parents TEACH cooperation.

This chapter will help you develop the skills for teaching cooperation with your children. To do this, we will need a few problems.

The Beauty of Problems

One of the realities of life — whether at home, at work, or in the community — is that problems will arise. Jesus himself warns, "In this world you will have trouble" (John 16:33, NIV). This is true for successful people, just as it is true for those who are unsuccessful. The difference is that those who succeed in our society are better able to handle problems effectively and to learn from them. Less successful people get bogged down in self-pity, play the blame game,

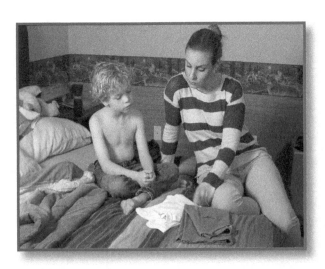

make excuses, and continue to make the same mistakes over and over again. Successful people seem to have the courage to cope with problems head on, enough self-esteem to believe they will find a solution, the responsibility to accept ownership of the problem, and the cooperative nature and respectful attitude to work with others in handling the problem. Where did they learn all of these problem-solving skills? Most likely they learned it through experience: from dealing with problems as children and then as adults, inside the family and out.

Our Christian faith also shapes how we deal with problems. Jesus's parable of two homebuilders can help us understand how:

> Therefore everyone who hears these words of mine and puts them into practice is like a wise man who built his house on the rock. The rain came down, the streams rose, and the winds blew and beat against that house; yet it did not fall, because it had its foundation on the rock. But everyone who hears these words of mine and does not put them into practice is like a foolish man who built his house on sand. The rain came down, the streams rose, and the winds blew and beat against that house, and it fell with a great crash. (Matthew 7:24-27, NIV)

Jesus compares the two homebuilders to illustrate that there is a vital difference between simply hearing the Word of God and putting the Word of God into practice. The man who built the foundation of his house in sand was all about taking the easier path. Digging into shifting sand is simple and quick. Though he must have known storms would eventually come, he didn't bother himself with such unpleasant thoughts. As a result, his house fell to the first big storm that came along.

The man who built his foundation in stone did think about the storms that would come, even though it was unpleasant to consider. And though building into solid rock takes time and diligence, progress is slow and the work is difficult, he did the work that was necessary to build a sturdy home that would stand against inevitable storms. He is called wise because he acknowledged the truth. The other man is called foolish because he ignored it.

The problems we will encounter in life are like the storms in this parable. We know that problems will eventually strike, and unless we build a strong foundation for ourselves and our children, those problems can wreak terrible damage. But building a strong foundation takes hard work and sacrifice, as the man who built his house on stone could attest. When things are going well in our lives, with no dark clouds visible on the horizon, it's difficult to keep working so hard and making those sacrifices, especially when we see other people taking short cuts, like the man who built his house on sand.

Faith gives us the peace of knowing that there is a reason for our hard work and sacrifice, and that taking the time and effort to build a strong foundation now will pay off in the future.

In the parable, Jesus emphasizes the vital difference between hearing God's Word and putting it into practice. Anyone can simply hear God's Word, but it takes something greater to move us to put it into practice. As Christians, we recognize that "something greater" is faith. It gives us the peace of knowing that there is a reason for our hard work and sacrifice, and that taking the time and effort to build a strong foundation now will pay off in the future. This makes the short cuts less tempting.

The rock on which we will build our foundation is made not only of our faith but also of the other qualities of character we introduced in Chapter 1: courage, responsibility, cooperation, respect, and self-esteem. The CAP problem-handling methods that we will be learning in this chapter incorporate all of these qualities. When we use these

methods mindfully, diligently putting into practice the wisdom of God's Word, our families will stand firm, not just weathering whatever trouble comes our way but actually growing from the experience.

Problems are a great resource for teaching. They are highly motivating, giving us a sense of urgency that overcomes our tendency to sit back and accept the status quo. Problems move lives forward. They help us grow. So when a problem occurs, the Christian Active Parent will take a deep breath and recognize that in spite of the inconvenience involved, a wonderful teaching opportunity has just become available. With three simple words, you can share this gift with your children:

Solve the problem.

Problems are a great resource for teaching. They are highly motivating, giving us a sense of urgency that overcomes our tendency to sit back and accept the status quo.

Straightforward as this request may seem, using it regularly with your children can open their eyes to a new philosophy of life, one full of opportunities to learn. To help you take advantage of these opportunitie, much of this book is organized around the concept of handling problems. We will begin by looking at ways you can build a cooperative relationship with your children and skills for helping them learn to solve problems. In later chapters, we will present discipline skills that can help you solve problems of misbehavior with your children. Communication will be a key in both cases as we continue to stress the need for participation and mutual respect in handling problems successfully.

First, let's take a look at the Christian Active Parenting "Problem-Handling Model" to get an overview of how this all fits together. The skills that make up this model will be presented in this and the next two chapters.

The Problem-Handling Model

Anticipate and prevent problems through problem-prevention talks
and other family meetings (see chapters 2-4).

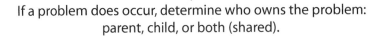

If a problem does occur, determine who owns the problem:
parent, child, or both (shared).

Parent-owned	Shared	Child-owned
Provide discipline.	**Provide discipline and support.**	**Provide support.**

Determine the child's goal and negative approach. Then avoid paying off the misbehavior.	Refer the problem to a family meeting.	If appropriate, allow natural consequences to teach.
		Let the child handle the problem, but offer support through Active Communication.

Basic Discipline
(Less-structured)

- Polite requests
- "I" messages
- Firm reminders

Advanced Discipline
(More-structured)

- Logical consequences
- FLAC method

*And no matter who owns the problem, pray for God's guidance
and encourage, encourage, encourage!*

Who Owns the Problem?

The first step in handling problems is to determine who "owns" the problem — that is, who should have responsibility for handling the problem.

Parent-owned Problems: With problems related to misbehavior, the parent as leader in the family owns responsibility for finding a solution. The discipline skills on the left side of the Problem-Handling Model can be used to find a solution in these cases. We'll address these skills in Chapters 3 and 5.

The first step in handling problems is to determine who "owns" the problem — that is, who should have responsibility for handling the problem.

Child-owned Problems: There are many problems that children encounter in their lives that are not really their parents' responsibility. These problems are "owned" by the child, and the child has the right to decide how to handle them. Of course, when our child owns the problem, we don't just ignore the situation or say, "It's not my problem." We offer support and take the opportunity to teach problem-solving skills and cooperation. These support skills are listed on the right side of the model.

Shared Problems: Sometimes problems are shared by the parent and the child. In these cases, the parent can offer both support and discipline.

Determining who owns the problem may be a more important part of solving the problem than you might first realize. Kids are very sensitive to their parents trying to control every aspect of their lives. Dictators take on too many of their children's problems as their own, creating unnecessary power struggles and even rebellion. On the other hand, parents with a Doormat style take on too few problems and leave the child to struggle alone when a little cooperation could be a valuable teaching tool. Active Parents decide what to do by first determining who owns the problem: the parent, the child, or both.

To determine who owns a problem, ask the following questions:

- **Who is the problem behavior directly affecting?** Whose needs or goals are being blocked? Who is raising the issue or making the complaint? That person usually owns the problem.

- **Does the problem involve health, safety, or family rules or values?** If so, then the problem belongs to the parent.

- **Is the problem within reasonable limits for your child's age and level of maturity?** If not, then either the parent owns the problem or it is shared.

Notice that seeking help from God is part of the problem-handling process regardless of who owns the problem. Our need to receive guidance from God is built into the very fabric of our existence. In Jeremiah 29:12-14 (ESV), the Lord declares, "You will seek me and find me, when you seek me with all your heart. I will be found by you." Though much in life may be uncertain, we can always trust the guidance God provides. So when a problem emerges in your family, no matter if you own it, your child owns it, or it's shared, asking for God's guidance is an important part of the problem-handling process.

Though much in life may be uncertain, we can always trust the guidance God provides.

Look at the chart on the next page for some examples that will help you better understand the concept of "who owns the problem".

To summarize what we have learned about problems:

1. Problems can be learning experiences.
2. When a problem occurs, determine who owns it.
3. If the parent owns the problem, use discipline skills.
4. If the child owns the problem, use support skills.
5. If the problem is shared, use discipline and support skills.
6. No matter who owns the problem, seek guidance from God.
7. No matter who owns the problem, always look for opportunities to encourage, encourage, encourage.

Situation	WHO OWNS THE PROBLEM?	Why?	What to do?
Children are talking loudly in the worship service at church.	Parent	The children are distracting you and others around you, interrupting your worship. Their behavior is disruptive and disrespectful.	Discipline Pray for guidance to discipline wisely.
Your child rides her bike on a busy street.	Parent	This problem involves the child's safety. It is the parents' responsibility to teach and enforce safety rules.	Discipline Pray for guidance to discipline wisely.
Your daughter doesn't like her sister going into her room without asking.	Child	Siblings are entitled to have a relationship with each other without parents interfering. The sisters need to learn how to work together and get along.	Support for both children Encourage children to pray for guidance or pray with them.
Your child complains that his teacher picks on him.	Child (Unless the teacher is clearly abusive)	Children have relationships with other adults. They need to learn how to relate to them on their own.	Support (If abuse or other serious problems exist, the parent needs to intervene.) Encourage child to pray for guidance or pray with him.
Your child has a temper tantrum in the supermarket.	Parent	The child's behavior is interfering with the parent's goal of shopping, as well as that of other shoppers.	Discipline Pray for guidance to discipline wisely.
Your six-year-old complains that he is being picked on by ten-year-olds.	Shared	This would be the child's problem, except that the age difference makes it beyond his level of maturity to handle.	Support for your child, intervention with the other children's parents Encourage child to pray for guidance or pray with him.
Your child is not keeping up with his schoolwork.	Shared	The parent's goal of the child being successful in school is blocked, yet school success is also the responsibility of the child.	Support and discipline Pray for guidance to discipline wisely.

Communication: The Road to Cooperation

Teaching a child how to solve problems cooperatively is in everyone's interest: the child's, the family's, the school's, the church's, and the larger community's. How we teach cooperation is a matter of how and what we communicate. It involves both attitude and skill.

Attitude: Christian Active Parents develop an attitude that says to the child, "You have the right to decide how to solve this problem. I can help, but you are the key to solving this and other problems you will encounter throughout your life. I believe you have what it takes to solve problems. You have good sense and a perspective that is truly your own. You will make some mistakes along the way, maybe some big ones. But you will recover from those mistakes, learn from them, and grow stronger in the process. Now, let's solve the problem."

Skill: Developing the communication skills to help others solve problems effectively will do more for your children than help them handle problems that they own. These same communication skills will continue to help them throughout their lives, making them better students, friends, workers, colleagues, and spouses. Why? Because communication skills help build cooperation skills.

Mixed Messages

Your message is carried on three separate channels: your words, your tone of voice, and your body language.

Developing an attitude of support is essential to building cooperation, because communication involves much more than just what you say. In fact, your message is carried on three separate channels:

Three Channels of Communication

1. **Your words**
2. **Your tone of voice**
3. **Your body language,** including hand gestures, how close you stand, and facial expressions

When it comes to communicating basic information like driving directions or a shopping list, your words carry most of the message. However, with an emotionally charged message like a problem, research has shown that more of the message is carried by body language, followed by tone of voice, and lastly, the words themselves. In other words, how you say something is often even more important than what you say.

When all three channels of communication carry the same message, the communication is very clear and powerful. However, when we say one thing with our words and something else with our tone and/ or body language, we send a *mixed message*. This not only dilutes the strength of the message, but often sabotages the spirit of cooperation you are trying to build. This is why developing a positive attitude is so important. If your attitude is negative, you may be able to hide it with the words you choose, but your tone of voice and body language will almost always give you away.

When all three channels of communication carry the same message, the communication is very clear and powerful.

Imagine that your child owns a problem and you have decided to let her handle it. You say, "I'm not angry. You can do whatever you think is best." However, your tone of voice, crossed arms, and scowl all say, "I'll be angry if you don't do what I think is best." This sort of mixed message makes it difficult for your child to know where she stands. An assertive child will probably hear the message she wants to hear and then do what she wants. A less confident child, however, may become anxious and confused about what to do. The key is to adjust your attitude so that you really accept her right to make the decision, even if her choice is not what you would prefer. You can also change your words to more honestly reflect your feelings. For example:

> *"I may be disappointed if you decide not to take your sister with you to the playground, but as I said, it's your choice and I can live with it."*

(Of course, your face and tone need to communicate this same message.)

In his second letter to the Corinthians, Paul poses a question in defense of his decision to change his travel plans: "Do you think I am like people of the world who say 'Yes' when they really mean 'No'?" (2 Corinthians 1:17b, NLT). He knew that clear and honest communication was a key to winning the Corinthians' cooperation. As Christian Active Parents, we share Paul's understanding that "As surely as God is faithful, our word to you does not waver between 'Yes' and 'No.' For Jesus Christ, the Son of God, does not waver between 'Yes' and 'No.'" (18-19). When our words, our tone of voice, and our body language are aligned, we communicate a clear "yes" or a clear "no" to our children. This consistent communication provides a stable foundation upon which our kids will build their own wise decision-making skills. James 5:12 (AMP) sums it up like this: "... let your yes be [a simple] yes, and your no be [a simple] no."

Mixed messages also erode discipline when the parent owns a problem. For example, you are reading a book when your child asks if he can stay up another hour to watch television. Your words say, "I don't think that's a good idea," but your tone and body language (as you continue to read your book) say, "I'm not really that concerned, and if you stay up, you probably won't get into trouble."

What do you think your child will do? Like most kids, he will use the confusion to do what he wants to do. Remember, when you split your message, you weaken your communication. The clearer you are, the more effective you are. Whether you're using discipline or supporting your child in solving a problem she owns, make an effort to keep your three channels of communication consistent.

Avoiding Communication Blocks

Most parents would like their children to feel free to come to them with their problems. Then we could help them solve these problems and eliminate the pain that such problems can bring. The trouble is that these very problems expose our children's self-esteem like a tender nerve. They may be extra sensitive to criticism, negative judgment, and other words or actions that seem to say that they are not worthwhile. These attitudes and behaviors can block communication with the child as effectively as a brick wall. If you are fortunate enough to engage your child in sharing a problem, you will want to guard against anything that might block communication and prompt her to withdraw.

communication block:

> Any words, tone of voice, or body language that influences a person sharing a problem to end the communication

When you listen and respond with an attitude of empathy and support, your child will begin to trust you with her feelings and share more of what is going on in her life.

When you listen and respond with an attitude of empathy and support, your child will begin to trust you with her feelings and share more of what is going on in her life. This sets the stage for you to influence her to make wise decisions. If you jump the gun and block communication, you will have lost this valuable opportunity to offer guidance and teach cooperation.

Look at the Communication Blocks chart on the pages 67-68. Each communication block in the left column represents a way that parents may disrespect a child's thoughts and feelings and instead focus on controlling the situation. More often than not, these attempts backfire. When relating to our kids, we do well to heed the advice of Matthew 7:1 (MSG): "Don't pick on people, jump on their failures, criticize their faults — unless, of course, you want the same treatment. That critical spirit has a way of boomeranging."

A child in pain needs to know that someone else feels the pain with her. The mistake parents often make is launching into an attempt to solve the problem for the child instead of supporting the child in solving the problem for herself. By trying to solve your child's problems, you may actually diminish her courage, self-esteem, and chance to learn how to solve problems cooperatively. Your goal should not be to provide a solution or to take away your child's pain; the goal should be to offer a caring ear, support, and encouragement, and to help your child find a useful solution for herself.

Ephesians 6:4 (NIV) advises parents: "... do not exasperate your children; instead, bring them up in the training and instruction of the Lord." It is exasperating and draining for children when parents block their communication. In contrast, the Lord's training and instruction is encouraging and life-affirming. Bring God into the discussion. Acknowledging that the Holy Spirit lives in each family member helps set the stage for constructive communication. The more you prayerfully consider God's opinion, the more fully you will be able to support your children's growing ability to make their own wise decisions.

The first step in learning to have a helpful discussion with your child without blocking communication is to identify the communication blocks you use most often. Be honest with yourself! Once you are aware that you use these blocks, be on guard the next time your child has a problem, and work hard to avoid exasperating your child by blocking their communication. When you find yourself using a communication block, catch yourself with a smile, apologize, and make a change.

Communication Blocks

Block	Example	Parent's Intention	What the Child Hears
Commanding	"What you should do is_____." "Stop complaining!"	To control the situation; to provide a quick solution	"You don't have the right to decide how to handle your own problems."
Giving advice	"I've got a really good idea..." "Why don't you _____?"	To solve the problem for the child	"You don't have the good sense to come up with your own solutions."
Placating	"It's not as bad as it seems." "Everything will be OK."	To take away the child's pain; to make him feel better	"You don't have a right to your feelings. You can't handle discomfort."
Interrogating	"What did you do to make him _____?"	To get to the bottom of the problem and find out what the child did wrong	"You must have messed up somewhere."
Distracting	"Let's not worry about that. Let's _____."	To comfort the child by changing the subject	"I don't think you can stand the discomfort long enough to find a real solution."
Psychologizing	"Do you know why you said that?" "You're being oversensitive."	To prevent future problems by analyzing the child's behavior and explaining his motives	"I know more about you than you know about yourself. Therefore, I'm superior to you."
Judging	"Why were you doing that in the first place?" "That wasn't a very smart thing to do."	To help the child realize what she did wrong	"You have poor judgment. You don't make good decisions."

Continued on next page.

Block	Example	Parent's Intention	What the Child Hears
Sarcasm	"Well, I guess it's just about the end of the world."	To show the child how wrong her attitudes or behavior are by making her feel ridiculous	"You are ridiculous."
Moralizing	"The right thing to do would be..." "You really should _____."	To reinforce your values with your child	"I'll choose your values for you."
Being a know-it-all	"Everybody knows that when something like this happens, you..."	To show the child that he has a resource for handling any problem — you	"Since I know it all, you must know nothing."
Focusing on mistakes	"I don't think you should have said that."	To help the child learn what she did wrong	"There is more wrong with you than right."
Negative expectations	"Now, don't blow it this time." "I know you won't remember to _____."	To get them to do the right thing with guilt or "reverse psychology"	"I have very little confidence in you." "Surely you couldn't get any worse."
Perfectionism	"If you had made all As, you wouldn't have to worry about it."	To motivate the child to do his best	"You are never quite good enough."

Active Communication

Instead of blocking communication and building a wall between you and your child, you can use Active Communication to build a bridge. This five-step process will help you teach your child cooperation and provide support. Active Communication is designed for times when your child owns the problem (or it is shared), and you want to help her find a good solution. You will find that the individual steps of the process can be used effectively in many other situations, as well.

Instead of blocking communication and building a wall between you and your child, you can use Active Communication to build a bridge.

The Five Steps of Active Communication

1. Listen actively.

2. Identify and respond to feelings.

3. Look for alternatives and evaluate consequences.

4. Offer encouragement.

5. Follow up later.

Let's take a look at each of these five steps:

1. Listen actively.

When you are listening actively, you do more than just receive information; you actively participate in the communication process. You listen with your eyes as well as your ears, keeping both focused on your child. You listen with your intuition as well as your intellect, using all available brainpower to address the situation at hand.

The goal of active listening is to encourage your child to share what he is thinking and feeling about whatever event is triggering the problem. Here's how:

Give full attention. Your child may feel encouraged by the attention alone. It says, "I care about you. You matter. I'm here to help."

Keep your own talk to a minimum. When your mouth is open, your ears don't work as well. So listen more, and talk less. Proverbs 18:13 (NIV) says it this way: "To answer before listening — that is folly and shame."

When your mouth is open, your ears don't work as well. So listen more, and talk less.

Acknowledge what you're hearing. Let your child know that you are taking his words to heart. You can say something as simple as "I see" now and then or even "Uh-huh." Ask questions to clarify, and after long stories give a quick summary to show that you are paying attention.

Listen with empathy. *Empathy* means sharing another person's feelings. Try to feel some of what your child is feeling, and show him with your tone of voice and facial expressions that you "get it." In short, listen for the feelings beneath your child's words and try putting yourself in his shoes. For example:

> *"Rhea, you look really down. What happened?" (Tone of voice and facial expression both showing concern.)*

> *"Jason, this must be hard for you. Let's talk." (Likewise, said with a concerned tone of voice and facial expression.)*

> *"Oh, Jenny... That must have really hurt." (Again, feeling the child's hurt and expressing your concern is the heart of empathy.)*

2. Identify and respond to feelings.

Most parents make the mistake of only listening to the facts of a child's story. While getting the facts straight is important, it is even more important to listen to what your child is feeling about her perception of the facts. There are three reasons why it is helpful for children to learn to acknowledge and accept their feelings rather than keep them bottled up:

1. When negative feelings are not expressed with words, they often get "acted out" through misbehavior. For example, a child who is scared and angry about his parents' divorce but has no one to share his feelings with may lash out in inappropriate ways without even knowing why.

2. The repression of painful feelings may lead some children to have emotional or even violent outbursts or suffer from stress-related ailments such as stomachaches, headaches, or bedwetting.

3. A child learning to describe how he feels and reflect on his feelings before making a decision is part of what is known as "emotional intelligence." People who learn to understand and manage their own emotions are better able to understand others' emotions. This aids them in all their relationships and provides a leg up when it comes to cooperating with others.

By listening this way, you will not only pick up a great deal of information; you will also communicate to him the most powerful message of all: that you care.

Unless your child comes right out and tells you what he's feeling, you will have to discover this yourself by listening closely to his tone of voice and watching his face, hands, and posture. By listening this way, you will not only pick up a great deal of information; you will also communicate to him the most powerful message of all: that you care. Recent research on brain development suggests that this "feeling of being felt" by another person is not only encouraging for children, but is actually instrumental in building important networks in their brains.

When you have an idea of what your child is feeling, reflect those feelings back to him. You become what psychologist Haim Ginott called an "emotional mirror." Mirrors don't judge how we look or tell us what to do; they just reflect what is there. Find a word or phrase that captures your child's feelings and connect them to what happened — the "content."

*"This is a really **scary** situation for you, isn't it, Rhea?"*

*"Jason, I know you are **angry** at me for being late."*

*"You're **worried** about what the other kids really think about your weight, aren't you, Jenny?"*

When you correctly name your child's feeling, an interesting thing happens: his head nods "yes," his eyes show recognition, and he continues talking. Your job at this point is to keep listening, empathizing, and reflecting back those feelings.

> *When you correctly name your child's feeling, an interesting thing happens: his head nods "yes," his eyes show recognition, and he continues talking.*

Rhea: *"Yes, it's scary. I don't know what I'm going to do."*

Jason: *"Yes! You said you'd pick me up right after practice."*

Jenny: *"I don't like it when they call me names."*

By reflecting feelings in tentative terms ("It sounds as though…"; "I guess…") you avoid coming across like you're trying to be a mind-reader or a know-it-all. If you miss the mark about what your child is feeling, he can correct you. That way you can be sure you understand what he is saying and feeling.

Rhea: *"No… I'm not scared. I'm mad! I hate it when those girls pick on weaker kids!"*

Mother: *"I see. You're really outraged!"*

By adjusting to your child's correction, the communication continues to flow. This opens a way for us to share God's Holy Spirit in our hearts with our children. Soon, God's love, peace, and wisdom will begin to permeate the daily interactions within our families.

3. Look for alternatives and evaluate consequences.

The first two steps of Active Communication create the right circumstances for solving problems. But since children usually don't spend as much time developing and evaluating solutions to their problems as mature adults do, we do not stop there. Until the executive part of the brain is fully developed, children are likely to choose the first solution that occurs to them, without pausing to consider other options or even the likely consequences of their first choice. A parent's role is to slow them down, help them look at various options, and predict the likely consequences of each.

You can move into step three by asking simple questions such as:

> *"What can you do about that?"*

> *"What else could you try?"*

After each alternative that your child comes up with, you can help her learn to predict possible consequences by asking:

> *"What do you think would happen if you did that?"*

Encourage your child to think of alternatives on her own, rather than pushing your ideas.

Encourage your child to think of alternatives on her own, rather than pushing your ideas. This helps her develop her own problem-solving skills and the persistence to keep thinking when solutions do not come easily. It also keeps her from being able to blame you if a solution does not work out well, which strengthens her sense of responsibility. However, if she does need prompting, you can gently suggest some ideas. Be careful not to take over or otherwise seem to insist that she do it your way. Remember, she owns the problem, and your role is that of a helpful consultant who makes suggestions but does not dictate solutions. You might simply ask, "Would you like to know what others have done in a situation like this?"

Sharing Your Experience: Another non-threatening way of introducing an alternative to your child is by sharing a story from your own experience. If you have faced a similar problem, you can share what worked or didn't work for you. For example:

> *"I don't know what you will decide to do, but that reminds me of a time when I wasn't invited to a party that I really wanted to go to. I sat around feeling hurt for a while, but then I decided that I wasn't going to let it ruin my whole weekend. So I found someone else in my class who wasn't going to the party and invited her to play at my house on that day. We spent the day together having a great time, and I made a new friend, too."*

Be careful not to turn this into a lecture of the "when-I-was-child-I-walked-five-miles-through-the-snow" type. Remember that your child must feel free to use or not use your ideas as she thinks best. Unless her solution is unsafe or violates your family values, it's best for you to remain accepting even if she chooses an alternative that you think will fail. After all, she owns the problem. Plus, there is a lot to be learned from failed ideas.

4. Offer encouragement.

Your child may or may not be ready to commit to a course of action at this point. (Remember that even Albert Einstein often needed time to let new ideas incubate before he made his decisions.) Either way, your encouragement can give your child the courage to follow through with action. For example:

> *"That sounds like a good idea to me. Let's see how it works out."*

> *"Like I said, I don't know what you will decide to do, but you're a smart kid and you'll think of something."*

> *"I really like your attitude about this."*

> *"You are really thinking this through. Nice going!"*

5. Follow up later.

You and your child can learn a lot by talking about how the problem turned out. First, ask how she handled the problem. Then ask what results followed. For example:

"How did it go with _____?"

"Remember that talk we had about _____ the other day? I was wondering how it turned out."

This follow-up helps your child learn from the experience and validates that your interest was genuine. If the results were good, then a little encouragement from you is all that is required. For example:

"That's great! I'm glad it worked for you."

However, if the results were poor and the problem still exists, or if new problems were created, then you can begin the Active Communication process over again with Step 1 to help your child find another solution. For example:

"Well, that's disappointing. I'm sorry it didn't work out. Let's see what we can learn from this. Then we can talk about what to do next."

Putting Active Communication to Work

Look for opportunities to use Active Communication to help your child solve her own problems. You'll find that the more supportive you are, the more cooperative your child is likely to be. Even if she is not willing to sit down for a long discussion, you can still listen, respond to feelings, and express your empathy. For example:

"You sure look down."

"I guess you're really ticked off."

You can even use these skills when disciplining or saying "no" to your child. Just having feelings recognized and accepted can sometimes help reduce a child's anger and improve cooperation. For example:

"I know you're angry that I won't let you go."

"I can live with you not liking me very much right now, but I don't think I could live with myself if something terrible happened to you."

Whenever you use Active Communication to help your child with a problem, remember that "God is our refuge and strength, a very present help in trouble" (Psalm 46:1, NIV). We handle problems within our families more effectively when we seek God's help first and keep ourselves grounded in the Lord's guidance.

Feeling Words

As you practice looking for the right words and metaphors to describe and mirror your child's feelings, you'll find that your "feeling word" vocabulary increases and the job gets easier. Use the following list of feeling words to help you get started.

PLEASANT Feelings		UNPLEASANT Feelings	
accepted	hopeful	afraid	jealous
adventurous	important	angry	let down
calm	joyful	anxious	lonely
caring	loved	ashamed	overwhelmed
cheerful	peaceful	defeated	rejected
comfortable	playful	disappointed	resentful
confident	proud	embarrassed	suspicious
eager	relieved	frustrated	uncomfortable
encouraged	secure	hopeless	unloved
glad	successful	hurt	unsure
happy	understood	impatient	worried
King of the world		Down in the dumps	
Like a million dollars		Walking on eggshells	
On the right path		Like a volcano about to erupt	

Quiet Time with God: Dealing with Your Own Feelings

We've emphasized that effective communication with children often hinges on how closely we pay attention to their feelings. In the spirit of caring for the caregiver, you also need to pay attention to your own feelings. Negative feelings such as anger, frustration, disappointment, fear, and anxiety are good fodder for prayer. Just as you want your children to come to you with their problems, God wants to hear your problems. 1 Peter 5:7 (NIV) encourages: "Cast all your anxiety on him because he cares for you." As we learned in Chapter 1, spending quiet time with God allows us to empty our feelings from our heart before being filled up with God's peace and perspective.

Noticing your own feelings will let you know when it is time to look deeper and share with God. Do you find yourself with shortened patience or quick to raise your voice? Do little things cause your temper to flare or easily invite negative feelings and thoughts into your mind? When we work out our own feelings by spending time with God, we become more patient, more kind, and more loving as listeners. We become a healthy sounding board for our children as they learn to identify and to express their own unique feelings. If we do not cast all our anxiety and other negative feelings on God, we might unintentionally cast them on our children. If we are overwhelmed with our own feelings, we will not be good listeners or clear "emotional mirrors" for our children.

If you have doubts about whether God really wants to know what you are feeling, remember the truth of 1 John 3:20b-21 (CEV): "God is greater than our feelings, and he knows everything. Dear friends, if we feel at ease in the presence of God, we will have the courage to come near to him." And heed the wisdom of James 4:8 (NIV): "Come near to God and he will come near to you." When troublesome feelings fill your heart, cast your burden onto God rather than passing it on to your children.

Family Enrichment Activity: Bedtime Routines and "I Love You"s

Children, particularly young children, want and need a lot of structure in their days. Knowing that certain things happen at certain times and in certain ways offers a sense of security and order to their worlds. As they get older, they can develop their own structures and depend on us less.

As with most things, moderation is a key. A rigid structure that can never vary (think "Dictator") is just as bad as a structure that is so flexible that children never know what they can count on (think "Doormat"). Christian Active Parents understand the benefit of routine and order but are also able to be flexible when the circumstances call for it.

Knowing that certain things happen at certain times and in certain ways offers a sense of security and order to children's worlds.

One of the best structures you can develop for your children is a bedtime routine. Many parents experience conflict at bedtime, but it doesn't have to be that way. Bedtime can be one of the happiest times of the day for both you and your children — if you make it fun and involving and keep these three tips in mind:

1. **Make it a win/win for both of you.** You can help make the bedtime routine more acceptable to your children if you look for ways to involve them in it and build in some parts that make it fun. This makes going to bed more desirable for kids and cuts down on conflict for the parents.

2. **Let the routine provide the discipline.** Of course, some kids may still resist parts of the routine, but this is where the fun parts can help provide the discipline. Remind the child that **all** parts of the routine have to be done in order or it's right to bed. For example:

   "If you are not willing to take a bath tonight, then you can go right to bed. Of course, we'll miss out on our story and other stuff, but it's your choice.

   (In Chapter 3 we will talk about this and other discipline methods that can help influence children's behavior.)

3. **Encourage…encourage…encourage.** Look for opportunities to point out what your child is doing well, what you appreciate, and to otherwise build on strengths. This both motivates and helps build cooperative behavior. We can recognize encouragement as a gift from God:

> **"May our Lord Jesus Christ himself and God our Father, who loved us and by his grace gave us eternal encouragement and good hope, encourage your hearts and strengthen you in every good deed and word."**
>
> *2 Thessalonians 2:16-17 (NIV)*

When we tap into God's deep reservoir of loving grace and eternal encouragement, our hearts are strengthened so that we may pass that encouragement and hope on to our children in everything we do and say. (We'll delve into the important subject of encouragement in Chapter 4.)

Here is a good bedtime routine that has been successful in many families with young children:

Bath Time: This is a good way to start the routine because if you make bath time fun, children can experience it as a continuation of play time. So add some bathtub toys and a little play, and have fun yourself. For example:

"Here's the world famous diver getting ready to do a triple somersault into a tub of wet children."

Teeth Brushing: Right after bath time is a good time for teeth brushing, which may never qualify as fun, but getting your children involved and using some encouragement can at least keep them on the right track. For example:

"You're doing such a good job getting to those teeth hiding way in the back."

Bedtime Story: One of the most fun parts of the bedtime routine is story time. Whether you read from a book or make up your own story, this offers a pleasant transition from the active play of the day to the quiet of bedtime. One way to encourage a child who is reluctant to read is to begin a longer book, reading one chapter each night. This gives the child something to look forward to each evening. With older children, you might substitute some quiet talk about the events of the day instead of a story. Whatever you do during this "talk and hug time," it's an opportunity for winding down and relaxing.

Prayer and Other Special Rituals: Include in your bedtime routine a reading from an age-appropriate Bible. (There are a wide variety of Bibles written for all age levels.) Read a Bible story or verses from Scripture that relate to a feeling or an event from your child's day, and then talk with your child about what you read. Reading and discussing segments from a children's Bible teaches your kids about Jesus and the way that he lived and loved. By incorporating Bible reading into your family's bedtime routines, you may set into motion what could become a child's lifelong love for Scripture and a close relationship with God.

Then it's time for lights out and your own special rituals. This might include a back rub, a Bible verse, a special poem, or a favorite song. For example:

"If all the little girls in the whole wide world were laid side by side and I could choose any one of them to be my daughter, I'd choose you."

End the bedtime routine with a time of heartfelt prayer. You and your child may choose to kneel by the bed, hold hands, or simply bow your heads together. You may want to ask your child to recite a favorite bedtime prayer, or you can recite it together. Then take turns giving thanks to all of the blessings in your lives. The details of how you and your child pray are, of course, up to you. What matters most is that your prayer is sincere.

It should be noted that if you and your child have had a rough day and are still angry at bedtime, it's important that you make an earnest effort to bring closure to the issue before lights out. Discussing it in a calm, loving manner, not an angry rant, will be more likely to produce positive results with your child. While this won't always succeed, it can often help your child rest well, knowing that you care. Ephesians 4:26 (NLT) reminds us: "Don't sin by letting anger control you." And don't let the sun go down on your anger. These are wise words for healthy relationships of all kinds. We will be discussing parenting and anger in depth in Chapter 5.

Expressing Love

> **"See what great love the Father has lavished on us, that we should be called children of God! And that is what we are!"**
>
> *1 John 3:1 (NIV)*

Building a positive relationship with children is an ongoing process and it takes steady effort. As we have seen, it involves making time to have fun together, using Active Communication, and showing mutual respect. Most of all, a positive relationship between parent and child involves expressing love for each other and sharing with one another the genuine love of God. Ephesians 5:1-2 (MSG) explains it well:

> Acknowledging and celebrating this great love is an essential part of Christian life: Watch what God does, and then you do it, like children who learn proper behavior from their parents. Mostly what God does is love you. Keep company with him and learn a life of love. Observe how Christ loved us. His love was not cautious but extravagant. He didn't love in order to get something from us but to give everything of himself to us. Love like that.

*Our children need
to know that
whatever happens,
whatever they do,
we love them and
God loves them.*

All children hunger for unconditional love, even those who seem to make a career of acting "unlovable." When children sense ifs or buts in their parents' love — "I love you IF you get good grades" … "I love you, BUT your whining drives me crazy" — they cannot feel comforted by the love that is offered. They are more likely to feel anxious, resentful, or just sad. Our children need to know that whatever happens, whatever they do, we love them and God loves them. As parents, we can weave loving gestures into their everyday lives in countless ways: a kiss, a pat on the back, a tousling of hair, an arm around the shoulder, a warm hug. But it is equally important to be able to tell them in words: "I love you" and "God loves you."

Showing "I love you": A Generous Helping of Hugs

Touch is your child's first language. From being cradled, warm and safe, nine months inside a womb to being

laid newborn upon a mother's breast, children are hard-wired to respond positively to loving touch and to recoil from dangerous touch. When children get enough hugs and other positive touches they are more likely to thrive. Without them they may not even survive.

The importance of hugs and positive touch is now supported by science. A warm, nurturing hug sends a signal to the child's brain, resulting in the release of the chemical *oxytocin*, which not only helps bond the child with the hugger, but also can help heal feelings of isolation, loneliness, and even anger. Think about the phrase, "Do you need a hug?" and all it communicates. We intuitively know that a well-meaning, compassionate hug can make us feel better. Holding a hug for twenty seconds or more can boost serotonin levels, increasing feelings of well-being and happiness. No wonder children who receive a lot of hugs are more likely to have high self-esteem, greater empathy for others, and even stronger immune systems.

Bottom line: Be generous with your hugs … and don't be afraid to throw in an "I love you" along with them. How many? That's up to you, but I recommend starting out with at least four a day. A hug in the morning, another one upon returning home from school or work, and again at bedtime are three that can become easy habits. Then add one more that suits you. Add as many as you like, if it feels right to you and your child. And while you're at it, make sure that you hug your spouse or significant other, and your good friends, as well. After all, you can use a hug, too.

Saying "I love you": Three Little Words

When is a good time to say those three magic words? Any time. Parents can say, "I love you" when the child will be surprised at the timing, but pleased with the message. Parents can say "I love you" at the end of a heated discussion, anchoring the problem-solving process in the truth that God's love remains stable at the heart of our family. Parents can say "I love you" at a time of calmness or tenderness, such as bedtime, and the child can bask in the warmth of the sentiment. These three words may come awkwardly for some parents, but the important thing is how beautiful they sound to children.

Ephesians 4:14-16 (MSG) tells us how God calls us to love: "God wants us to grow up, to know the whole truth and tell it in love — like Christ in everything. We take our lead from Christ, who is the source of everything we do. He keeps us in step with each other. His very breath and blood flow through us, nourishing us so that we will grow up healthy in God, robust in love."

As Christian Active Parents, the love we share with our children comes from tapping into Christ's deep reservoir of love for all of humankind. Even when our own personal resources are depleted, we can dig deep within to find that reservoir, and from that source we can nourish our families with love. Scripture captures it best:

> "Love is patient, love is kind.
> It does not envy, it does not boast, it is not proud.
> It does not dishonor others, it is not self-seeking,
> It is not easily angered, it keeps no record of wrongs.
> Love does not delight in evil but rejoices with the truth.
> It always protects, always trusts, always hopes,
> always perseveres. Love never fails."
>
> *1 Corinthians 13:4-8a (NIV)*

Remember, we communicate through three channels: words, tone of voice, and body language. It is important that we use all three of them when we say "I love you." When we build the foundation of our family on the limitless love of God, we will be able to stand firm as we face life's storms, winds, and rising waters.

Family Meeting: Bedtime Routines

Take a few minutes this week to discuss your family's bedtime routine with your children. Let them help determine how it will go, keeping in mind our guiding principle of "freedom within limits." You, as the parent, still have the responsibility to determine matters of health and safety, so leaving out teeth brushing, for example, is not an option. However, whether to brush her teeth before or after her bath, whether she should brush her upper or lower teeth first, or what flavor toothpaste to use are choices your child can help to make. Put "the method of choice" we learned in Chapter 1 to good use!

Be sure to cover some of the following questions during your meeting:

■ What time is lights-out for each child? Will you allow a period of quiet reading after lights out?

- What is the routine? (Be sure to include reading the Bible together as well as your child's choice of age-appropriate reading material.)

- What happens if the routine is broken? For example, will the child have to go straight to bed, as mentioned, or go to bed fifteen minutes earlier the next night?

Make sure that you "listen actively" and "identify and respond to feelings" (Steps 1 and 2 of Active Communication) during the meeting. After all, part of the point of family meetings is to show children that their parents care about them, and are not there just to lay down a bunch of rules. Also, it's a good idea to write down the routine your family comes up with and post it in your child's bedroom or bathroom as a reminder. Finally, if you do not already enjoy the ritual of putting your child to bed, but instead see it as a chore, try to enjoy it just a little more. For example, as a creative way to express the love of God to your children, teach them a favorite song or Bible story you remember from your own childhood. Bedtime can really be a very special time of the day for you, too, so don't miss out on this mutual blessing.

3: Responsibility & Discipline

> *Patrick had never had a job, and though he was 27 years old, his parents were still supporting him. But finally the day came when they'd had enough of his dependency, as well as their own overprotection. They gave him three months to find a job. Patrick didn't take the threat seriously at first, but when he saw after ten weeks that his parents were not bluffing about pushing him out of the nest, he began looking for work in earnest.*
>
> *Even so, he failed. No one had ever taught him the value of doing things for himself, and he had never developed the skills to find a job. His father, as usual, came to his rescue. He called a friend in the construction business who arranged for Patrick to have a job as a carpenter's assistant. On the first day of his first job, Patrick was reprimanded for taking a two-hour lunch break. The next morning he got an earful from the foreman for leaving tools outside overnight (Patrick had figured that someone else would collect them.) But the incident that got him fired was on the second day, when he backed a dump truck into the side of the house they were building. The foreman confronted Patrick and asked why he was even driving the truck, since he wasn't authorized to do so and he had only been asked to bring in some supplies. Patrick replied, "Well, I thought it would be easier than carrying all that stuff myself. Besides, nobody told me not to."*

This chapter will present methods of handling problems and misbehavior when they occur in a family. But it is also about something much more basic to the development of a child's ability to survive and thrive in our modern society. It is about responsibility.

The concept of responsibility comes up again and again in the Bible. As our maker, God is responsible for humankind, and God's message to us is clear:

"... the God who created the cosmos, stretched out the skies,
laid out the earth and all that grows from it, Who breathes life
into earth's people, makes them alive with his own life:
I am GOD. I have called you to live right and well.
I have taken responsibility for you, kept you safe."

Isaiah 42:5-6 (MSG)

In turn, we humans owe responsibility to God, because without
God's gift of creation, we would be nothing and have nothing. Our
responsibility to God calls us to live right and well. And when we
bring children into the world, we are obligated to teach them about
their responsibility and to keep them safe as they grow into their own
God-given ability to survive and thrive responsibly.

God has not left us alone to take on the challenging responsibility of
parenting. As we shepherd our children through the myriad choices
and consequences of life, God is doing the same for us parents. The
Lord is our own personal shepherd, as the well-known verses of the
23rd Psalm tell us:

"The Lord is my shepherd, I shall not be in want.
He makes me lie down in green pastures.
he leads me beside quiet waters, he restores my soul.
He guides me in paths of righteousness for his name's sake.
Even though I walk through the valley of the shadow of death,
I will fear no evil, for you are with me;
your rod and your staff, they comfort me.
You prepare a table before me in the presence of my enemies.
You anoint my head with oil; my cup overflows.
Surely goodness and love will follow me all the days of my life,
and I will dwell in the house of the Lord forever."

Psalm 23 (ESV)

A shepherd's role is one of much responsibility: he guides and directs; he leads the flock to good pastures; he teaches its members to stay together; he rescues those who have wandered off and are lost; he protects the flock from danger. It is a great comfort to envision God watching over us, shepherding us as we shepherd our children. Parenting may not always be easy, but if we give ourselves to God and do good work, we will receive the guidance we need to raise our children and care for our families.

What is responsibility?

We can usually recognize responsible behavior when we see it. The young man in the opening story lost his job because he was not behaving responsibly. But what does the word "responsible" really mean? For Christian Active Parents, it means three things:

1. Accepting one's obligations

2. Doing the right thing as the situation calls for it

3. Accepting accountability for one's actions

1. Accepting your obligations

Given a choice, children will usually choose to do what they *want* to do over what they *do not want* to do. As obvious as this might seem, it is important to acknowledge that part of maturing is learning to postpone gratification. There are times in all of our lives when we would rather not do something we feel obligated to do. Responsible parenthood, for instance, is filled with times when we sacrifice our own immediate desires for the long-term benefit of our families. Helping your child understand the need for occasional self-sacrifice is part of teaching him responsibility. That means doing what you are obligated to do before (or instead of) doing what you would really like to do. Meeting one's obligations is a cornerstone of success in any society.

Helping your child understand the need for occasional self-sacrifice is part of teaching him responsibility.

Some of these obligations are made consciously between people: when you tell your child that you will pick her up after school, you are obligated to be there. Other obligations are made implicitly through the roles we accept in our daily lives. The job of parenting, for example, carries with it many obligations including providing food, clothing, shelter, discipline, and support. When a responsible person is unable to fulfill their obligations, they feel bad and work hard to correct the situation. They don't just blow it off. Teaching our children that there are times when we must sacrifice our own short-term desires for long-term benefits is teaching them responsibility. Childhood is filled with opportunities to teach this lesson. For example:

Owning a pet means accepting responsibility for caring for it.

Being on a team means showing up for practice and games.

Taking music lessons means practicing.

Being in a family means doing chores.

Being a student means doing homework and studying.

Volunteering means showing up on time and doing the work that is needed.

Sometimes fulfilling an obligation is not fun. It's OK to acknowledge that. In fact, when your child has to pass up something fun in order to meet an obligation, acknowledging that it's a bummer can help him feel better about his sacrifice. For instance, let's say he has to refuse a party invitation because he has already committed to volunteering at a church function that day. Let him know that you realize it would be more fun to go to the party, but it takes courage to pass up some of the fun stuff in life for the sake of an obligation, and his responsible attitude will pay off in the long run.

2. Doing the right thing as the situation calls for it

Helping our children learn the difference between right and wrong is part of our job as parents. As children earn the freedom to make decisions by themselves, they also take on the responsibility to do what is right in any given situation. This is not always easy. For example, most adults would readily agree that it is right to obey the law, and that we should teach our children to do so. Yet when Dr. Martin Luther King, Jr. broke Alabama's segregation laws during the Civil Rights Movement, we recognized his actions as not only responsible, but also as morally courageous. Over time, people came to discover that the laws were wrong and Dr. King was right.

As children earn the freedom to make decisions by themselves, they also take on the responsibility to do what is right in any given situation.

Of course, we must be careful that our children do not take from that lesson the idea that breaking the law is OK in any general sense or that any person is above the law. Sometimes we have to impose our own limits to our freedom. The fact that we *can* do something does not mean we *should*. Paul wrote of this to the Corinthians as he encouraged them onto a path of righteousness:

> **"'I have the right to do anything,' you say — but not everything is beneficial."**
>
> *1 Corinthians 6:12 (NIV)*

Doing the right thing is often a lot like spelling. For every rule there seems to be an exception. For example:

> *Do not hurt others...unless it's in self-defense.*
>
> *Do not lie … unless it's a white lie to spare feelings.*
>
> *Work hard … but don't be a workaholic.*
>
> *Stand up for your friends … unless they are doing something wrong.*

Taking time to talk with your children about real-life situations is the best way to help them grapple with the many nuances of right and wrong. Asking them, "What do you think is the right thing to do?" implies that in your family you strive to know what is right and to do it. The Corinthians quote above provides a key to determining whether a choice is right for the situation. Encourage your child to ask himself, "Is it beneficial? And for whom?"

At the very core of responsibility is the idea that what happens to you is the result of decisions you make.

When your child does the right thing, be sure to encourage her by acknowledging both the action and the courage it took to act. When your child does the wrong thing, help her understand why it was wrong and what she could do differently the next time.

3. Accepting accountability for your actions

In the Bible, as soon as God creates human beings, the blame games begin. Blaming is Adam's first response in the Garden of Eden when God catches him and Eve overstepping the limits of the freedom God gave them: "The woman you put here with me — she gave me some fruit from the tree, and I ate it" (Genesis 3:11b-13, NIV). Adam not only blames Eve, but also subtly points the finger at God for making Eve his companion.

At the very core of responsibility is the idea that what happens to you is the result of decisions you make. Rather than accept this, it is much easier for some people, including children, to blame their problems on other people or circumstances, or just to make excuses. But doing so prevents them from learning to make better decisions in the future. After all, if it wasn't their fault, why should they think about what they could do differently next time? Of course, there are sometimes circumstances beyond one's control. But even then, we still have choices about how we can improve those circumstances, and that is where responsibility comes in.

When children accept responsibility for what happens to them, they learn to prevent or solve their own problems.

For example, when Lisa's grades began dropping, she blamed it on her teachers for being boring. This thinking is not likely to help her improve her grades, since she can't control her teachers to make them more interesting. But what if she took responsibility for the situation and said to herself, "There's a lot of boring stuff in this class, but I want to do well in school, so I'd better study harder anyway. What can I do to make it more fun?" When children accept responsibility for what happens to them, they learn to prevent or solve their own problems.

You can think of responsibility as a formula:

$$R = C + C$$

Responsibility = Choice + Consequences

This formula covers all three aspects of responsibility, since "Choice" includes the choice to meet or not meet one's obligations and the choice to do right or wrong. It's part of a parent's job to help our children learn that their choices have consequences. This is one of the most empowering lessons they can learn, in or out of the classroom.

How can you help your child develop responsibility?

First, recognize that children often avoid responsibility because of how parents and other adults treat them when they own up to their mistakes and misbehavior. Often their reward for taking responsibility is to be hurt with blame, punishment, and shame. Most people learn early in life that if they can make a good excuse or blame someone else for their mistakes and misbehaviors, they can avoid being hurt. So, the first step in helping your child learn responsibility is to avoid hurting her when she makes a bad choice. Try not to discourage her further through put-downs, punishments, or other disrespectful forms of discipline.

Next, teach your child the relationship between her choices and the consequences that follow by using discipline techniques that are neither hurtful (the Dictator's approach) nor missing altogether (the Doormat's approach). Remember, the Christian Active style of parenting is based on the concept of "freedom within limits." This means allowing your child the freedom to make choices within limits that are appropriate for her age and level of responsibility. The better your child handles her freedom of choice, the more freedom you allow her in the future. Who sets these limits? Sometimes the parents, as leaders in the family, set them, often with input from the child. Sometimes they are set by outside groups your child is involved with, like schools, churches, or clubs. Learning to live within the limits of any given situation is kind of like participating in a sport: playing within the rules is almost always the clearest path to success. After all, there are usually consequences for playing *outside* the rules.

Learning to live within the limits of any given situation is kind of like participating in a sport: Playing within the rules is almost always the clearest path to success.

Finally, to help your children develop responsibility, you need to model responsible behavior yourself. Determining how well you're doing in this area might require some soul-searching. Galatians 6:4-5 (MSG) advises: "Make a careful exploration of who you are and the work you have been given, and then sink yourself into that. Don't be impressed with yourself. Don't compare yourself with others. Each of you must take responsibility for doing the creative best you can with your own life."

Reward and Punishment Often Backfire

Discipline is important for teaching how to live within the limits of a situation. However, discipline does not necessarily mean reward or punishment. In fact, the word itself comes from the Latin word, *disciplina*, which means, "to teach." The word *disciple*, a person who sits at the feet of a teacher and learns, comes from the same root. How we choose to teach our children right from wrong, the importance of fulfilling their obligations, and accepting responsibility for their actions can have a lasting impact.

We mentioned earlier that the Dictator enforces his orders by doling out rewards and punishments. He keeps children in line with the threat of punishment if they misbehave and the promise of reward if they do what he wants them to do. This system of reward and punishment may have been effective in older days when the world was ruled by kings, queens, and emperors, and everyone "knew his place," but in a society of equals, it doesn't work very well.

reward:

> Something out of the ordinary that the child likes, used either as a payment for past positive behavior or as a bribe to motivate future positive behavior

The following story helps illustrate the problem with rewarding good behavior:

> *As a young man, Active Parenting author Michael Popkin spent some of his summers as a director at a boys' camp. Being a student of "behavior modification" at the time, he decided to see if he could teach a cabin of campers to say "thank you" for the milk and cookies he gave them at bedtime without outright asking them to say it. On the first night, he passed out the goodies and observed as each camper took his handout without a word. Finally, as the last camper took his cookie, he said, "Thank you." Promptly Michael rewarded that camper with another cookie and said, "You are welcome." The following night Michael decided to start with this camper so he might demonstrate what he had learned for his cabin mates. When Michael gave him his carton of milk and cookie, the boy quickly put them aside then held out his hand again, saying, "Thank you, thank you, thank you, thank you…"*

In a society based on equality, a reward for good behavior comes to be expected as a right. A child does not learn to behave cooperatively just because the situation calls for it, or because the family functions better when everyone follows the rules or pitches in. Instead, he develops a "what's in it for me?" attitude that leads him to expect more and more rewards for positive behavior. It can become downright inflationary!

Rewards and punishments have no place among equals. Only a superior can give rewards and mete out punishments, and only inferiors can receive them.

The poor parent must then increase the value of the reward to keep it effective, until she reaches a point of frustration. This frustration often leads to the use of punishment.

punishment:

A method designed to hurt a child, either physically or psychologically, in order to teach the child what not to do in the future

There was a time when teachers thought that the best way to discourage students from giving wrong answers in class was to rap them across the knuckles with a ruler. This method was smartly abandoned when conventional wisdom realized it didn't work as a teaching technique, and what was more, it also produced unwanted side effects.

Punishment, whether it's physical (like a spanking or mandatory push-ups) or psychological (like shaming or taking away privileges), continues to be a popular way for parents to deal with their children's misbehavior because it often works in the short run. However, in the long run, hurting children in order to teach them positive behavior makes no more sense than smacking them with a ruler for saying that 1 + 1 = 3. It's bad policy.

Remember those side effects mentioned above? When you hurt someone in a society based on equality, the hurt party becomes resentful. Not only that, but they also tend to conclude that they have the right to hurt you back. Children in this position — remember, their brains are still under development, and they lack the full supply of morality — will often get their revenge through misbehavior that is much worse than what they did wrong in the first place. They know what their

parents value and can hurt us where it matters most. And if nothing else works, they can hurt us through their own failure.

In fact, rewards and punishments have no place among equals. Only a superior can give rewards and mete out punishments, and only inferiors can receive them. All in all, rewards and punishments as methods of child rearing are holdovers from an earlier time. There are much more effective methods of discipline, and we will be learning about many of them in this chapter. But first we need to address one of today's most controversial discipline issues.

To Spank or Not To Spank?

> "He tends his flock like a shepherd:
> He gathers the lambs in his arms
> and carries them close to his heart;
> he gently leads those that have young."
>
> *Isaiah 40:11 (NIV)*

This beautiful passage, another appearance of the shepherd analogy in Scripture, gives us a sense of how deeply God values the young and serves as a model for how we are to care for our children. Throughout Scripture we can find examples of Jesus modeling a loving care for children and treating them with great respect: "But Jesus called the children to him and said, 'Let the little children come to me, and do not hinder them, for the kingdom of God belongs to such as these'" (Luke 18:16, NIV). It is fitting that we followers Christ show our children the same love and respect.

That's not so hard when children are behaving well, but when they misbehave, it can be a real challenge to maintain the loving and respectful attitude that God wants us to have. Once we let anger and frustration start influencing our choices, we are more likely to resort to harsh words, spanking, and other punishments instead of constructive discipline. Many of today's parents were themselves raised with these methods, and they might argue that they turned out fine. But in our modern egalitarian society, that punishing kind of discipline will do much more harm than good for children. And as Christians, we know that no form of violence against children is justified.

The Shepherd's Rod

In biblical times, the job of a shepherd was necessary and important, and the shepherd's rod was the tool upon which the flock's survival depended. With the rod, a skilled shepherd could direct the flock, guide wayward sheep back to the fold, and drive off predators. The rod came to represent strength, authority, and guidance.

The Bible contains many references to the shepherd's rod as an instrument of discipline and guidance. Remember the line from Psalm 23, "Your rod and your staff, they comfort me." God, as the Good Shepherd, uses his shepherd's rod to guide the flock of humankind. And just as the Lord is our shepherd, parents are their children's shepherds. The rod we wield to guide our children is discipline.

Unfortunately, the idea of the rod as a parenting tool is sometimes used in a way that can be harmful to children. The old maxim "spare the rod, spoil the child" is often cited as evidence that the Bible promotes spanking to force children's compliance. This phrase is actually not a direct quote from the Bible. Proverbs 13:24 (NKJV) states, "He who spares his rod hates his son, but he who loves him disciplines him promptly." With our broadened understanding of the shepherd's rod, a different interpretation emerges: "Sparing the rod" means failing to guide the child or protect him from danger. It is "hateful" in the sense that such neglect could cause the child harm. The loving approach is to use the "rod of discipline" promptly to guide and to protect the child. As parents, in our role as shepherds to our children, we use the "rod of discipline" to express love and to comfort, to redirect and guide. We do not use the shepherd's rod to hit or to hurt.

As parents, in our role as shepherds to our children, we use the "rod of discipline" to express love and to comfort, to redirect and guide. We do not use the shepherd's rod to hit or to hurt.

As we encourage the development of character and responsibility in our children, Christian Active Parents use the "rod of discipline" in the true spirit of the word *discipline*: to teach rather than to punish. What's more, we encourage the growth of our children's faith and the joy of living closer to God.

"Come to Me...", an original oil painting by Helen Wiejackzka from the altar at St. Mary's Church, Wappingers Falls, NY, commissioned by Catherine Cwiakala in memory of her mother, Grace Faas

8 Reasons Not to Spank Your Child

Spanking is a high-risk method of discipline, sort of like driving without a seatbelt: You may get away with it, but why take the chance? To elaborate, here are eight good reasons not to spank.

1. **It is not biblically sound.** The Gospels are full of accounts of Jesus rejecting violence in favor of love, even for people who saw Him as an enemy. That doesn't mean He let people off the hook when they behaved badly. He addressed it through teaching rather than using punishment, shaming, or physical aggression. Jesus spoke passionately about the rightness of protecting and caring for people who are small and vulnerable, especially children. He also showed love by healing the sick and afflicted with His touch. Children, in their innocence, had a special significance to Jesus, as His words in Matthew 18: 5 (NIRV) remind us: "Anyone who welcomes a little child like this in my name welcomes me."

2. **It is easy for an enraged parent to cross the line from spanking to abusing.** The adrenaline rush that venting one's frustrations and anger on a child can produce is a "high" that can become addictive. Unfortunately, by the time the smoke clears many parents have crossed the line from spanking to hitting, shaking, slapping, and other forms of child abuse. This is why even parent educators who advocate spanking say to NEVER spank while you are angry. Calm down before you approach your child or decide how to handle the problem.

3. **Spanking usually leads to more misbehavior.** A big problem with spanking is that it does work ... for the immediate misbehavior. Kids will "stop it this instant!" However, they also resent the spanking, and afterwards they will seek out conscious or unconscious ways to get even.

4. **Spanking models aggressive behavior.** Kids that are spanked learn to handle problems with violence or the threat of violence. Others find that their parents are too big to get even with, so they take it out on other kids. We have to teach kids that violence is only OK as a measure of restrained self-defense and never as a way to "punish" others for misbehavior.

5. **Spanking can damage your relationship with your child.** When you spank, often you create a climate of hurt and revenge that undermines much of the good in the relationship. Why take this chance when there are better methods available?

6. **Spanking is out of step with the times.** Since the 1950s, the number of parents in the U.S. who spank has dropped from over 95% back then to 50-60% in recent years. Even the American Pediatric Association has come out against spanking.

7. **Spanking often leaves the parent feeling guilty.** Even before the societal shift in spanking trends, many parents sensed that something was not right about hurting a child "for his own good," and they felt guilty afterwards. Parents can't act with confidence when they intuitively know that their actions are off the mark.

8. **If spanking worked, parenting would be easy.** Most people agree that parenting well is difficult. That's why parent education is needed. Michael Popkin tells a story about visiting the San Diego Zoo with his family. They stopped to observe the gorillas. A mother gorilla was eating when a child gorilla began annoying her. She simply took a massive arm and backhanded the misbehaving child across the compound. It doesn't take a high level of intelligence to hit a child. If it worked, then parenting would be easy, not difficult, because we could all do it. There must be more to effective discipline in our complex democratic society than there is in the primitive society of apes.

Effective Discipline and the Problem-Handling Model

In Chapter 2, we discussed the importance of using problems as teaching tools for instilling qualities of character such as cooperation, courage, responsibility, and respect in our children. We saw how using effective communication skills promotes cooperation while teaching how to solve problems. Let's take another look at the Problem-Handling Model that we presented in that chapter. Look at the model on the next page. This time we're focusing on the left side of the chart, which shows methods of handling parent-owned problems with effective discipline methods. But more important than just handling problems, these methods teach responsibility.

The Problem-Handling Model

Anticipate and prevent problems through problem-prevention talks and other family meetings (see chapters 2-4).

If a problem does occur, determine who owns the problem: parent, child, or both (shared).

Parent-owned

Provide discipline.

Determine the child's goal and negative approach. Then avoid paying off the misbehavior.

Basic Discipline (Less-structured)

- Polite requests
- "I" messages
- Firm reminders

Advanced Discipline (More-structured)

- Logical consequences
- FLAC method

Shared

Provide discipline and support.

Refer the problem to a family meeting.

Child-owned

Provide support.

If appropriate, allow natural consequences to teach.

Let the child handle the problem, but offer support through Active Communication.

And no matter who owns the problem, pray for God's guidance and encourage, encourage, encourage!

The rest of this chapter explores how to use discipline skills to teach your child responsibility and how to live within the limits that you determine as family leader. When using any of the discipline skills that follow, keep these tips in mind:

Let discipline be motivated by caring. When a child knows that you are disciplining her because you care about her, it's easier for her to accept

- **Your goal is to teach your children, not to hurt them.** Remember, discipline comes from *disciplina*, to teach. We can teach far better without hurting their feelings or their bottoms.

- **Whenever you discipline a child for negative behavior, find opportunities to encourage any improvement the child makes in the future.** Your encouragement will do a lot to promote more positive behavior. On the other hand, when a child improves behavior after being disciplined and you ignore the improvement, it can be very discouraging. And discouragement leads to misbehavior.

- **When using discipline to influence your child, use the least assertive method that works.** Research suggests that the less a child attributes his positive behavior to outside forces (your discipline), the more he internalizes the reason for his positive behavior as his own. This leads him to develop positive values, which will promote positive behavior, even when you aren't around to offer discipline.

- **Let discipline be motivated by caring.** When a child knows that you are disciplining her because you care about her, it's easier for her to accept. When we discipline out of frustration, anger, and our own desires, it's difficult for the child to accept or learn the lesson we're trying to teach.

And finally, keep in mind that although disciplining your child is not the most enjoyable of your responsibilities as a parent, the payoff will be well worth the effort. With practice and patience you'll find that CAP discipline skills really do work. Both parents and children will be able to appreciate the results. Trust in Paul's words from Hebrews 12:11 (NIV): "No discipline seems pleasant at the time, but painful. Later on, however, it produces a harvest of righteousness and peace for those who have been trained by it."

Basic Discipline Methods

The first three discipline methods we'll present are basic communication skills that increase in assertiveness from mild to firm. Start with the first, and if it doesn't work, move on to the second, and then the third. They are:

Polite requests

"I" messages

Firm reminders

Polite Requests (vs. Harsh Orders or Silent Wishes)

Asking your child politely for what you want is often enough to influence him to change his behavior, especially if your relationship is already a positive one.

Not every problem or conflict requires firm discipline or a lot of discussion. Asking your child politely for what you want is often enough to influence him to change his behavior, especially if your relationship is already a positive one.

When your child doesn't know what you want in a situation, your first step is to politely make your desires known through a request. After all, children are not mind readers. For example, you have decided that you no longer want to pamper your child by picking up the dirty dishes he leaves in the den. Your polite request might be:

"Honey, from now on will you do me a favor and bring your dirty dishes to the sink when you're through with your snack?"

If your child agrees, be sure to add,

"Thanks. That will be a big help."

This may seem so simple that it sounds ridiculous, but sometimes that's all a child needs. Of course, you could let it simmer inside for another week until you're really fed up, then burst out with, "I'm sick and tired of having to pick up your mess! What do you think I am, your servant? If you weren't so lazy and inconsiderate ..." However, this is not likely to produce responsibility, cooperation, or dishes in the sink (at least not on a regular basis).

If at first your child does not comply with your polite request, offer a friendly reminder:

> *"I noticed you forgot to put your dishes in the sink. Please come get them."*

"I" Messages (vs. "You" Messages)

If your child repeatedly forgets to keep an agreement or continues the problem behavior, you'll need a stronger message. "I" messages are firm and friendly communications that can produce surprisingly effective results. Psychologist Tom Gordon called them "I" messages in his pioneering program, Parent Effectiveness Training (P.E.T.), because they shift the emphasis from the child (a traditional "you" message) to how the parent ("I") feels about the child's behavior.

"I" messages:

- allow you to say how you feel without blaming or labeling.

- make it more likely that your child hears what you are saying because you say it in a respectful manner.

- tell your child how her behavior affects others (your feelings).

- put the emphasis on your child's behavior rather than his personality.

■ give your child clear information about what change in behavior you want.

When to Use an "I" Message

"I" messages are effective only when the parent owns the problem — when you have the responsibility and authority to decide on the solution. Since "I" messages work best when delivered in a firm, calm tone of voice, avoid using them when you are too angry. Allow time to cool off, then approach your child when you have regained control. An angry "I" message can easily trigger a power struggle.

How to Send an "I" Message

There are four parts to an "I" Message:

1. **Name the behavior or situation you want changed.** In order to avoid attacking your child's self esteem, it's important to "separate the deed from the doer." It isn't that your child is bad, only that you have a problem with something he is doing. By beginning with a statement aimed at the behavior, you avoid triggering a power struggle.

   Begin by saying either, "I have a problem with ..." or "When you ..." For example:

   "I have a problem with you leaving dirty dishes in the den."

   "When you leave dirty dishes in the den ..."

2. **Say how you feel about the situation ...** and say it without raising your voice. This lets your child know that the problem is serious to you. Although parents often use the word "angry" to describe their feelings, this frequently masks other emotions, mainly fear and hurt. Kids are less defensive and better able to hear us when we express these and other less threatening feelings, instead of always

relying on anger. "I feel concerned" or "I feel hurt" may be both closer to the truth and more effective in many cases. For example:

> *"I feel taken advantage of …"*

3. **State your reason.** Nobody likes to be treated as if he were a robot and expected to be blindly obedient. If you're going to change what's comfortable to you to please someone, you at least want that person to have a good reason for asking you to make the change. Children feel this as strongly as adults do. A simple explanation about how your child's behavior is interfering with your needs can go a long way. For example:

> *"… because I have to spend time and energy cleaning up after you."*

Remember, you get more of what you ask for than what you don't ask for.

4. **Say what you want done.** You've already made a polite request or two, so now you're getting more assertive. This means letting the child know exactly what you'd like done. Remember, you get more of what you ask for than what you don't ask for. This step can begin with "I want" or "I would like." For example:

> *"When you leave the den, I want you to bring your dirty dishes to the kitchen and put them in the dishwasher."*

Putting this "I" message all together, we have:

> *"I have a problem with you leaving dirty dishes in the den. I feel taken advantage of because I have to spend time and energy cleaning up after you. When you leave the den, I want you to bring your dirty dishes to the kitchen and put them in the dishwasher."*

Making "I" Messages Stronger: Two Variations

1. **Getting agreement:** *"Will you do that?"*

You can make an "I" message even stronger by getting an agreement from your child about the behavior you want changed. This can be done by simply adding the question, "Will you do that?" and then maintain eye contact and don't move until you get a "yes." Saying "yes" verbally commits the child to action and helps motivate her to follow through later. You can also do this by changing the last step of the "I" message from "I would like …" to "Will you please …" For example:

> *"I have a problem with you leaving dirty dishes in the den. I feel taken advantage of because I have to spend time and energy cleaning up after you. When you leave the den, I want you to bring your dirty dishes to the kitchen and put them in the dishwasher. Will you do that?"*

2. **Establishing a time frame:** *"When?"*

Every parent knows the frustration of getting an agreement from a child about doing something, finding it still undone hours later, and confronting the child only to hear the refrain, "I'll do it." The implication, of course, is "I'll do it when I get around to it," and that may not occur while you are still young enough to care. Your solution is to get a clear agreement as to when the behavior will be completed. In the above example, the "when" is built into the phrase "when you're finished?" Or you can simply ask, "When?" right after your child agrees to the request.

Firm Reminders

Changing habits is not easy for anyone. Your child has gotten used to whatever behavior you are trying to change, and even with good intentions, he will probably sometimes forget. Other times he may test to see if you are really committed to the change by sliding back into the old negative behavior. In either case, your next step is to give a short but firm reminder. By suspending the rules of grammar and syntax, you give the message additional "oomph." For example:

"Dishes. Sink. Now."

The fewer words you use, the better. Avoid the temptation to give a lecture on responsibility. Just make solid eye contact and firmly remind your child about what you want done — and when. Your child may very well spring into action, amazing you and surprising himself in the process. If so, build on this success by encouraging him with a "thank you." Even if he is less than enthusiastic, focus on his positive behavior at this point, and not his negative attitude. For example:

Parent: *"Dishes, sink. Now."*

Child: *"Whatever." (Said as he slowly gets up and slouches towards the kitchen, dirty dishes in hand.)*

NOT THIS:

Parent: *"WHAT'S YOUR PROBLEM?! I DON'T SEE WHY YOU CAN'T DO A SIMPLE THING LIKE PUT YOUR *&%*$ DISHES IN THE SINK WITHOUT MAKING A HUGE DEAL ABOUT IT! IS THAT TOO MUCH TO ASK?!"*

THIS:

Parent: *"Thanks. I appreciate it."*

Your encouragement may eventually help change his attitude to match his behavior. So keep it positive.

Advanced Discipline Methods

When basic discipline methods do not solve the problem, you can turn to more advanced skills:

■ Natural and logical consequences (covered in this chapter)

■ The FLAC method (covered in Chapter 5)

Natural Consequences

Remember that a key aspect of responsibility is accepting that what happens to us is a result of our choices.

Responsibility = Choice + Consequences

It stands to reason, then, that to teach your child responsibility for her actions, you must give her the freedom to make choices and let her experience the consequences of those choices. Kids learn a lot about what works and what doesn't from the consequences of their actions. There are two basic types of consequences: natural and logical.

In Christian Active Parenting, we define "natural consequences" this way:

natural consequences:

The results that occur from a child's behavior without any interference from a parent or other authority

Examples of natural consequences:

The natural consequence of forgetting to wear a jacket is getting cold.

The natural consequence of staying up late on a school night is oversleeping and being late for school the next day.

The natural consequence of leaving a bicycle outside may be that it gets rusty or that it is stolen.

Natural consequences are powerful teachers. We have all learned important life lessons this way. Natural consequences work well as teachers because they allow the parents to act as a sympathetic third party, rather than the disciplinarian.

In order for natural consequences to be effective, avoid two temptations:

1. Don't rescue your child *on a regular basis* from the natural consequences of his actions.

2. Don't say, "I told you so" or otherwise lecture your child about her mistake. It's better to say, "Gee, honey, I know that's frustrating." Then let the natural consequences do the teaching.

When You Can't Use Natural Consequences to Teach

There are three circumstances in which a responsible parent cannot allow Mother Nature to take her toll:

1. **When the natural consequence may be dangerous.** The natural consequence of playing in the street may be getting hit by a car.

2. **When the natural consequence is so far in the future that the child is not concerned about it.** The natural consequence of not brushing your teeth may be that you develop cavities months or years later.

3. **When the natural consequence of a child's behavior affects someone other than the child.** The natural consequence of allowing your kids to be rowdy at a restaurant is that it bothers other diners as well as you.

Logical Consequences

In cases in which you cannot rely on natural consequences to teach your child responsibility, you'll need to set your own consequences. In order to teach your child that he is responsible for his choices, the consequence that you set needs to be logically related to your child's misbehavior. For this reason, we call these "logical" consequences.

logical consequences:

> Discipline, provided by a parent or other authority, which is logically connected to misbehavior, to teach a child to behave within the limits of a situation

Examples of logical consequences:

> *When Sean repeatedly forgets to bring his dirty dishes into the kitchen after snacking in the den, he loses the privilege of taking food out of the kitchen.*

> *When Maria posts inappropriate messages on a website, she is not allowed to use the Internet for a week.*

Logical consequences are very different from punishment, even though the child probably won't like either. Some of the differences are:

Logical Consequences	Punishment
logically connected to the misbehavior	not connected to the misbehavior
intended to teach responsibility	intended to teach obedience
given in a firm and calm way	often delivered with anger and resentment
respectful	disrespectful
allow the child to participate	dictated by authority

Dennis The Menace ® used by permission of Hank Ketchum and © by North American Syndicate.

How to Use Logical Consequences

Many parents unintentionally turn a would-be logical consequence into a punishment, and then they wonder why their child responds uncooperatively. To be sure you're giving a logical consequence and not a punishment, follow these guidelines. It may seem like a lot to remember at first, but as you practice, it will become second nature.

Guidelines for Using Logical Consequences

1. Ask your child to help decide the consequence.

2. Put the consequence in the form of a choice:
    either/or choice   **when/then choice**

3. Make sure the consequence is logically connected to the misbehavior.

4. Give choices you can live with.

5. Keep your tone of voice firm and calm.

6. Give the choice one time, and then enforce the consequence.

7. Expect testing (it may get worse before it gets better).

8. Allow your child to try again after experiencing the consequence.

1. Ask your child to help decide the consequence.

You stand a much better chance that your child will cooperate with you if you include her in the decision-making process.

Since the Active style of parenting is based on respect and participation, it is wise to ask your child to help decide the consequences of her misbehavior. You stand a much better chance that your child will cooperate with you if you include her in the decision-making process. You might also be surprised how often she comes up with choices and consequences that you wouldn't have thought of on your own. On the other hand, kids will often respond with typical punishments (grounding, push-ups, and the like) rather than logical consequences. So you'll need to explain that the concept of logical consequences is a tool to help them learn, not a punishment to make them sorry. For example:

> *"Katy, I still have a problem with you leaving your things all over the house. What do you think we can do to help you remember to clean up after yourself?"*

Even if your child doesn't give you any helpful suggestions or is uncooperative about finding a solution, it is important that you asked. Since you have invited her participation, she will be less likely to think of you as a Dictator and to rebel against the consequence.

2. Put the consequence in the form of a choice.

Logical consequences teach responsibility, which means "choices plus consequences." Therefore, always present your logical consequence in the form of a choice. Your child can choose positive behavior with a naturally occurring positive consequence, or she can choose to misbehave and have you provide a logical consequence.

Try one of these types of choices:

> **Either/or:** *"Either _____ or _____. You decide."*

> **When/then:** *"When you have _____, then you may _____."*

Either/or choices are best used when you want to influence your child to stop a negative behavior. For example:

> *Katy leaves her stuff scattered around the house in the afternoon.*

> *"Katy, either put your things away when you come home from school, or I'll put them in a box in the basement. You decide."*

Notice that the logical consequence of leaving her belongings lying around is the inconvenience of having to dig them out of a junk box in the basement.

> *Carter regularly forgets to put his dirty clothes in the hamper.*
>
> *"Carter, either put your dirty clothes in the hamper, or wash them yourself. You decide."*

In this example, the logical consequence of Carter continuing to leave his dirty clothes on the floor is the work of doing his own laundry.

When/then choices are best used when you want to influence your child to start a positive behavior. They take two events that already occur and order them so that the child must do what you want her to do before she is allowed to do what she wants to do. This is not a bribe or reward, because both behaviors are a normal part of the child's life already.

Examples of when-then choices:

> *Selina has trouble getting her homework done but spends a lot of time surfing the Internet.*
>
> **Yes:** *"Selina, when you have finished your homework, then you may get on the Internet."*
>
> **No:** *"Selina, if you do your homework, you may use the computer an hour longer than usual tonight."*

(That last one is a reward, not a logical consequence, because it offers the child something extra for a task she should be doing anyway. Remember that rewards tend to become expected as a right, so we do not recommend using them.)

> *Tom is about to go to the swimming pool, but he has ignored his regular Saturday chore of mowing the lawn.*

Yes: *"Tom, when you've mowed the lawn, then you may go swimming."*

No: *"Tom, you may not go swimming until you have mowed the lawn."*

(By putting it in the negative like this, the parent makes it sound like a threat. Since threats tend to lead to power struggles, we do not recommend that parents use them.)

3. Make sure the consequences are really logical.

Logical consequences must be logically connected to the child's misbehavior or else they are just punishments presented as a choice. Kids in a democratic society are very sensitive to injustice, whether real or perceived. When your consequence is logical, they will be much more likely to see it as fair, even if they complain.

Not Logical	Logical
"Either come to dinner when I call you or lose the privilege of watching TV for a week."	"Either come to dinner when I call you or eat it cold."
"Either share the computer with your brother or you're not going out on Saturday."	"Either share the computer with your brother or neither of you will be able to use it tonight."
"Finish your homework or you're grounded."	"When you finish your homework, then you may play your video game for half an hour."

Tip: There are many logical consequences that will work for any given problem, but thinking of them does not always come easily, especially if you're accustomed to using a few basic punishments like grounding for every problem. With practice, logical consequences will begin to come to you more easily. It will help to brainstorm logical consequences for specific problems with your partner, a close friend, or with other parents in an CAP group.

4. Give choices you can live with.

If you give your child a choice, you have to be willing and able to live with the consequences of whichever choice he makes. If you are not comfortable with the consequence, you are likely going to undermine it, so it will not be effective.

If you give your child a choice, you have to be willing and able to live with the consequences of whichever choice he makes.

For example, in an Active Parenting group, a mother suggested this logical consequence for a problem she was having with her son:

> *"Either put your dishes in the dishwasher, or I will let them sit in the sink until you do."*

The group leader wisely asked the parent if she could live with a sink full of dirty dishes, at which point the mother admitted that it would drive her crazy. The group helped her come up with a better consequence for the misbehavior — one that she could live with:

> *"Either put your dirty dishes in the dishwasher or anyone in the family can do it for you and you can pay them $2 each time for the service. You decide."*

Another parent solved the same problem with this logical consequence:

> *"Either put your dirty dishes in the dishwasher or when we run out of clean dishes, I'll serve dinner without them!"*

It only took one dinner of spaghetti and meatballs served on a bare table to teach the lesson. Of course, not many parents could live with that consequence, but it goes to show that there are many possible logical consequences a parent can think up, so be creative and patient, and do what feels right for you and your family.

5. Keep your voice firm and calm.

When you give a choice, and later when you enforce the consequence, it's important that you remain calm and use a firm tone of voice. An angry tone of voice (the autocratic parent's pitfall) invites rebellion

and a fight. At the other end of the spectrum, a wishy-washy tone of voice (the permissive parent's pitfall) tells your child that you don't really mean what you say, which also invites rebellion. A firm and calm tone by an authority figure says, "I will treat you respectfully, but you are out of bounds here. My job is to help you learn to stay in bounds, and I plan to do my job."

6. Give the choice one time, then act.

For a logical consequence to be effective, you must enforce it. If your child continues to misbehave after you have given him a choice, immediately follow through with the consequence. Do not give the choice a second time (or a third and fourth time!) without putting the consequence into effect. If you continue to repeat yourself, you are just training him to ignore you until you get angry. Your child must see that his choice results in a consequence and that you mean what you say. You don't want to be harsh about it, but you do want to consistently enforce the consequence. For example:

> *"If your books were in the kitchen when I cleaned, then you will find them in the junk box in the basement."*

7. Expect testing.

Many children test their parents' commitment to the logical consequence they've presented. *Will Mom really take my toys away if I leave them in the living room again?* Kids "test" to see if we are consistent. So expect that the misbehavior may even get worse before it gets better.

If you consistently enforce the consequences you set, in time your child will see that her testing isn't weakening you, and at that point

If you consistently enforce the consequences you set, in time your child will see that her testing isn't weakening you, and at that point she'll probably improve her behavior.

she'll probably improve her behavior. After all, kids don't do what doesn't work. But until then, try to avoid getting angry if your child tests you. Just continue enforcing the consequence firmly and calmly.

Tip: In some cases you might observe that your consequence just doesn't matter much to your child. This isn't testing; it's a form of informal "deal making." For example, when Jared hits his little brother, his mother enforces the logical consequence of sending him to his room for an hour. She reasons that this is a logical consequence because if Jared can't be around other people without hitting, then he shouldn't be around other people at all for a period. But while he's in his room, Jared thinks, *"Being in my room isn't so bad. I have my* Legos™*, my crayons, my action figures ... what else could I need? Plus, that little brat really gets on my nerves. He deserved a good smack. All in all, I'd say the price was well worth it."*

> *Try to avoid getting angry if your child tests you. Just continue enforcing the consequence firmly and calmly.*

If you suspect that your child is not motivated by the consequence you have set, then you'll either need to find a different consequence or attack the problem in other ways: a family meeting or the FLAC Method (covered in chapter 5.)

8. Allow your child to try again later.

Since you want your child to learn from the consequences of his choice, give him a chance to try again after he's experienced the logical consequence. For example:

> *Sondra has agreed to do her chores on Saturday before watching TV. On Saturday morning, her dad notices that Sondra's chores are still not done but she is parked in front of the TV, watching her favorite show.*
>
> *"Sondra, I noticed that you haven't done your chores yet. We agreed you'd do them before watching TV. That means no more TV today. You can try again tomorrow."*

If Sondra does her chores before tomorrow, she can watch her show then. If she doesn't, then she'll have to continue living without TV.

Tip: You may want to increase the length of time before the child gets to try again each time she repeats the misbehavior.

Logical consequences take a little practice to get used to and more practice to do well. If you find yourself having trouble coming up with appropriate logical consequences, try brainstorming with your spouse, significant other, or a friend. If you find that your child is slow to respond to your logical consequence, check it against the eight guidelines to see if you are accidentally turning a logical consequence into a punishment. If so, make your corrections and try again. Keep at it and you will find that logical consequences become easier and easier to use.

Hebrews 12:5-11 (MSG) asks a good question: "... have you forgotten how good parents treat children, and that God regards you as *his* children?" The passage continues with some wise words for parents:

> My dear child, don't shrug off God's discipline, but don't be crushed by it either. It's the child he loves that he disciplines; the child he embraces, he also corrects. God is educating you.
>
> He's treating you as dear children. This trouble you're in isn't punishment; it's *training*, the normal experience of children. Only irresponsible parents leave children to fend for themselves. Would you prefer an irresponsible God? We respect our own parents for training and not spoiling us, so why not embrace God's training so we can truly *live*? While we were children, our parents did what *seemed* best to them. But God is doing what *is* best for us, training us to live God's holy best. At the time, discipline isn't much fun. It always feels like it's going against the grain. Later, of course, it pays off handsomely, for it's the well-trained who find themselves mature in their relationship with God.

An Early Lesson in Logical Consequences

The following is paraphrased from Dr. Popkin's first appearance on the Oprah Winfrey show.

Oprah Winfrey: *"Dr. Popkin, how old do children have to be to use this discipline method?"*

Dr. Popkin: *"One time, when our first child, Megan, was about one year old, she stood up in her rocking chair. I told her that rocking chairs were for sitting and to please sit down. Not surprisingly, she just stood there looking at me with an expression that seemed to say, "What are you going to do if I don't?" I then offered her a choice: "Megan, you can either sit in the chair or I'll have to put it away." Again, not surprisingly, she stood there and stared at me. I calmly and gently picked her up and put her on the floor, then took the rocking chair outside the gated room. She just watched. The next day when she stood in the rocking chair I again said that she could either sit in the chair or I'd have to remove it from the room. She sat down. The lesson had been learned by a one-year-old."*

Family Meeting: Problem-Prevention Talks

Children often misbehave simply because they don't know what parents expect from them. They don't know where the limits are and how much freedom they are allowed.

Imagine how frustrating it would be to play a game of softball if you didn't know the rules. Rules are important for any activity, including day to day living in families. To prevent problems and get along well in a family, everyone needs to be clear about the rules and expectations.

Children often misbehave simply because they don't know what parents expect from them. They don't know where the limits are and how much freedom they are allowed. Of course, many a shrewd child will play dumb about the rules, figuring that "it's easier to gain forgiveness than permission." In either case, many problems can be prevented if you take the time to discuss guidelines and expectations before the situation occurs.

The CAP approach to problem prevention is not about laying down the law and dictating what the rules are. A much more effective approach is to discuss potential problems with your child and decide together what solution or guidelines the situation requires. Of course, as the parent you will have certain limits that are nonnegotiable, but a willingness to be flexible within those limits can go a long way to winning cooperation and avoiding problems. For example: You have some grocery shopping to do, and you need to take your five-year-old daughter with you. Having a short talk with your child before you leave home can improve the chances of your outing being problem-free, which could save you a lot of time and stress.

The following guidelines can help you make your Problem-Prevention Talk effective:

Guidelines for Problem-Prevention Talks

1. Identify potential problems and risks.

2. Share thoughts and feelings.

3. Generate guidelines for behavior.

4. Decide on logical consequences for violating the guidelines (if necessary).

5. Follow up later.

Let's go over these guidelines one by one. We'll use the shopping scenario as an example.

1. Identify potential problems and risks.

If you have been in similar situations before, then you probably know where the trouble spots will be. Otherwise, use your experience of similar situations and your knowledge of your child to anticipate the problems. For example, your child often whines for you to buy her things whenever she goes shopping with you. She also has a tendency to wander off, forcing you to chase after her.

2. Share thoughts and feelings.

Ask your child what she thinks about the situation and what problems might arise. You may be surprised that she also has concerns. Then make your own thoughts and feelings clear in a friendly manner. For example, your child may feel that grocery shopping is boring and she'd rather be outside playing. You might say that you understand that shopping is boring for her, but that you need to buy food for the family to eat.

3. Generate guidelines for behavior.

Using the information you gathered in step two, talk with your child about what you expect of her. When discussing guidelines, keep in mind that it will be easier for your child to comply with the rules if she feels like she is gaining something by doing so. We aren't suggesting the use of rewards or bribes for cooperative behavior, but including incentives can be effective. For example, avoid:

"If you're good, I'll buy you a toy."

This is a bribe or a reward, and will lead to having to buy the child something every time you go to the store and will also teach her to manipulate others.

BETTER:

> *"If we finish our shopping by 4:30, we'll have time to stop by the park on the way home."*

BEST:

> *"How would you like to help me do the shopping by handing me the groceries off the shelf? Maybe you can help me pick some things you'd like to have for dinner this week."*

> *"Great! I also need for you to stay beside me all the time so that you'll be safe and we won't interfere with other shoppers."*

4. Decide on logical consequences for violating the guidelines (if necessary).

Your child will be more likely to follow the guidelines if she knows there will be logical consequences if she violates one. You don't need to use this step with kids who are basically cooperative or who have not had problems in similar situations. In fact, such a warning may seem like an insult to a child who only needs to be included in the discussion and have her needs considered in order to cooperate. For more challenging kids, however, consequences are very helpful when done right. For example:

> *"When we get to the store you can either walk with me or ride in the cart."*

5. Follow up later.

In situations in which you are not around to ensure that the guidelines were followed, you will need to check up to see how your child behaved. If she has followed the guidelines, then you can encourage her by acknowledging the good effort. If she has not, then you will need to enforce the logical consequences.

Family Enrichment Activity: "Catch 'em Being Good"

Let's do a quick one-question experiment: Are you aware of the temperature where you are right now? Chances are that unless you are either too hot or too cold, you aren't thinking about the temperature. We rarely sit around thinking, "Gee, it sure is comfortable around here. I hope nobody messes with the thermostat or brings me a fluffy blanket." But let it get too hot or cold and see how our awareness levels shift. The same is true of our kids. As long as they are behaving well and doing what we would like, we often fail to notice. But let them misbehave and see what happens to our awareness!

This chapter has been about using discipline skills to handle parent-owned problems and, at the same time, teach your child responsibility. The skills we have presented are tools for you to choose from when discipline is needed. They are respectful and allow the child to participate in solving the problem, which teaches the important skill of self-discipline. Still, like all discipline methods, they fall short.

To really get the most out of discipline, you also need to pay attention to what your child is doing well.

To really get the most out of discipline, you also need to pay attention to what your child is doing well. When children get the idea that they are only noticed or important when they misbehave, what do you think they are going to do in the future? Misbehave. Christian Active Parents recognize that children need encouragement for positive behavior even more than they need discipline for negative behavior. They look for opportunities to "catch 'em being good" and then offer an encouraging word. This focus on the positive is especially important after you have used discipline to correct misbehavior.

This week, practice training yourself to notice more of the positive things that your children do, and comment on them in a supportive, affirming way. Here are a few phrases to get you started:

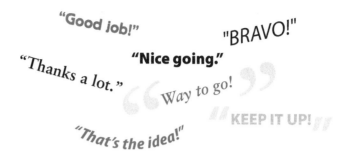

"Good job!"   "BRAVO!"

"Nice going."

"Thanks a lot."   "Way to go!"

"KEEP IT UP!"

"That's the idea!"

Feel free to build on this list as it suits you. For example, we saw how Dennis the Menace's mother used a logical consequence to teach her son not to paint on the walls. Let's say that a few days later she "catches him being good" and wants to offer him some encouragement. She can say something simple like:

> *"I really like the way you are using paper for your art project."*

This lets Dennis know that she recognizes the effort he has made to stay within the limits that she has set, and it will likely encourage him to cooperate more in the future.

If she is feeling more expressive, she can add something like:

> *"I feel good knowing that you heard what I said about not painting on the walls. Now you can create your fabulous artwork, and we can have clean walls, too. How about if we tape your pictures on this wall? It will be like having our own museum."*

You may recognize this structure as similar to an "I" Message. The difference is that with these positive "I" Messages we are focusing on the child's improvement or other behavior that we want to see more of in the future. You may notice that at the end, instead of telling Dennis what she would like him to do differently, she offers something he will probably like. (This is similar to a reward, which can often backfire, but is different enough that it is unlikely to produce a "what's in it for me?" attitude.)

Another example: After using your new discipline skills to decrease the fighting between your children, you catch them cooperating. Your positive "I" message might start out like this:

"I really appreciate how you two have worked on getting along better with each other. It makes me feel good to see you enjoying each other's company…"

At the end of your positive "I" message, you can let them know that their cooperation has let you get your work done faster, so now you have time to make some popcorn, play a game, or _____ (Fill in the blank with a fun activity that you and your kids choose together).

Don't worry if you don't use every step of the positive "I" message every time. The first statement alone (telling them what you like) is good encouragement by itself. And it's best to use your own words so that the message feels natural to you.

As we close this chapter, we leave you with this blessing:

"Now may the God of peace who brought up our Lord Jesus from the dead, that great Shepherd of the sheep, through the blood of the everlasting covenant, make you complete in every good work to do His will, working in you what is well pleasing in His sight, through Jesus Christ, to whom be glory forever and ever. Amen."

Hebrews 13:20-21 (NKJV)

4: Building Courage & Self-Esteem

▸ *Long ago, before the invention of convenience stores, a group of humans called "milkmen" wandered the earth in the early morning darkness delivering bottles of their precious liquid. In one of the neighborhoods they visited, there lived a 5-year-old boy who was afraid of the dark. Early one morning before the sun had risen, the boy's mother, hoping to help her child overcome his fear, encouraged him to open the front door and bring in the milk. He was afraid, but she persisted. "Go ahead," she said. "God is outside and He will protect you." The boy thought about that for a moment, and then moved his small hand toward the door. He fearfully turned the knob, reached his hand into that cold, dark morning, and shouted, "If you're out there, God, hand me the milk!"*

Preparing a child to courageously meet the challenges that life offers is one of the most important aspects of parenting. Courage is such an important character trait in today's complex world of choices that it forms the very foundation upon which a child constructs her unique personality. In fact, psychologist Alfred Adler and the great leader Winston Churchill both said that courage is the most important of all traits because it is the one on which all others depend.

Courage ... One from the Heart

We learned earlier that the French word *coeur*, meaning "heart," is the root of the English word *courage*. Just as the heart has long been considered the center of human emotions, courage might be thought of as the core of a person's character. It is the "heart" or "grit" that enables us to take reasonable risks, knowing that if we fail we will still be all right. And it is through risk-taking that we are able to develop responsibility, cooperation, independence, and whatever

Courage and Fear

Courage first met Fear
When I was still a child.
Courage gazed with cool, clear eyes;
Fear was something wild.

Courage urged, "Let's go ahead."
Fear said, "Let's turn back."
Courage spoke of what we had;
Fear of what we lacked.

Courage took me by the hand
And warmed my frozen bones.
Yet Fear the while tugged at my legs
And whispered, "We're alone."

Many have been the obstacles
Since first I had to choose,
And sometimes when Courage led me on
I've come up with a bruise.

And many have been the challenges
Since Fear and Courage met,
And yet those times I've followed Fear,
Too often—tagged along Regret.

- Michael H. Popkin

else we may strive to achieve. In fact, we define courage in Active Parenting like this:

courage:

> The confidence to take a known risk for a known purpose

Courage is a feeling. It is a feeling of confidence empowered by faith in God. It motivates us to take risks, knowing that we have a chance to succeed, and that even if we fail, the risk was worth taking. Courage is not the absence of fear, but the willingness to take a reasonable risk in spite of fear, knowing that God has our backs. Without this feeling of courage, we often find ourselves sitting on the sidelines, unwilling to take the risks inherent in any endeavor.

Without courage, we let life pass us by while we wait for someone else to "hand us the milk."

One of our greatest examples of courage is from the life of Jesus. His beliefs and the unflinching way He stood for them made Him a target of the powerful elite of his day, but fear of punishment did not make Him back down. Not even fear of death could do that. Jesus's death on the cross was not only the ultimate sacrifice for God's redeeming plan; it was also the ultimate act of courage.

We receive our courage to live a life of faith and character by keeping our eyes fixed on Jesus's courageous example. As Hebrews 12:1b-3 (NIV) encourages:

> Let us throw off everything that hinders and the sin that so easily entangles. And let us run with perseverance the race marked out for us, fixing our eyes on Jesus, the pioneer and perfecter of faith. For the joy set before him he endured the cross, scorning its shame, and sat down at the right hand of the throne of God. Consider him who endured such opposition from sinners, so that you will not grow weary and lose heart.

When we follow Jesus's example of obedience to God, we provide an example of a living, courageous faith for our children to follow.

Self-Esteem ... One from the Mind

Where does a child's courage come from? It comes from a belief in her unique self: the belief that she is a lovable, capable person who has a lot to contribute and a good chance to succeed. And even when she doesn't succeed, she knows that she is much more than just her achievements — that there is something worthwhile about her because God loves and accepts her as she is.

This belief — high self-esteem — helps motivate her to continue to work hard for good grades even after she has received a low one. It gives her the confidence to say "no" to her friends when they invite her to goof off instead of study, or even later in life when they pressure her to use drugs or engage in other destructive behavior. When self-esteem is high, we believe we have a reasonable chance to succeed and we know that all is not lost if we don't. We have the confidence to tackle life's challenges. We have courage.

High Self-esteem ➡ Courage

Unfortunately, the opposite is also true. When we think badly of ourselves, believing that we are unlovable or not capable, our self-esteem drops. This low self-esteem produces discouragement and fear.

Low Self-esteem ➡ Discouragement

Consider the high esteem with which God, the Supreme Parent, values each of us. In the Bible, Daniel relates a story of how, when he prayed for the courage to face a challenge, God appeared to him as the angel Gabriel and said, "Do not be afraid, you who are highly esteemed … Peace! Be strong now; be strong." Daniel continues: "When he spoke to me, I was strengthened and said, 'Speak, my lord, since you have given me strength.'" (Daniel 10:19, NIV)

If we can see ourselves as God sees us and value ourselves as God values us, if we can believe that God's Holy Spirit within will give us strength, then we will have self-esteem. God gifts us with belief in ourselves, activating the Holy Spirit within our hearts. As parents, we serve God when we help our own children develop self-esteem.

Can a child have too much self-esteem?

Self-esteem sometimes gets a bad reputation from people who see parents heaping praise on their kids for every minor achievement. Some of these children and adults seem to act as if they can do no wrong, or they are just plain self-centered and arrogant. Is this too much of a good thing or too much of the wrong thing?

We'd argue that such people have too much of the wrong kind of self-esteem. When a person's self-esteem is based solely on achievements (especially inflated achievements), praise from others, or a sense of entitlement, it is built on sandy soil that will easily crumble under pressure. Self-esteem is much more enduring when it is built upon stone: faith in God and strong character, a feeling of belonging to a community, growth and development as a person, and contributions to the common good. It can take a hit and get back up, knowing that success and failure do not determine a person's full value.

To belong. To learn. To contribute. These are the cornerstones of a foundation that will provide a real and lasting sense of self-esteem for a child. The spiritual root system that Christian faith provides will make it even stronger. You may think that being made in God's image (Genesis 1:26), having God's breath fill our lungs (Genesis 2:7), and being given the power of God's Holy Spirit (Acts 1:8) would be enough to provide a solid foundation of self-esteem and courage for all of God's children. Yet, the challenges we face in this world have a way of undermining our confidence. Often it takes encouragement from others to remind us of the value of our true, God-given selves.

To Belong

To Learn

To Contribute

The Think-Feel-Do Cycle

Let's take a look at how courage and self-esteem fit together in something we call the "Think-Feel-Do Cycle." It includes four separate parts: events (anything that happens in the child's life), thoughts (including his beliefs, attitudes, and values), feelings, and behavior.

The Think-Feel-Do Cycle

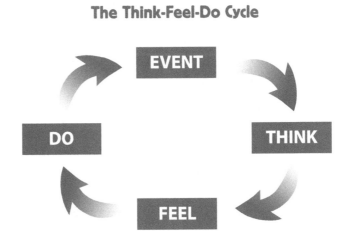

This is how the cycle works: When something happens to a child (an **Event**), it triggers thoughts, both conscious and unconscious (**Think**). All of his attitudes, beliefs, and values about similar situations and what he has learned come into play. This thinking then produces a feeling or emotion (**Feel**). Many people mistakenly believe that feelings just happen, but they are really products of our thoughts and values. Change the thinking and you change the feelings, too. Together, the thinking and feeling produce an action (**Do**). This action may have an effect on the event, which will trigger new thoughts, feelings, and behavior as the system goes around and around. For example:

Ten-year-old Steven's mother notices that he has left the milk out on the counter and says in an angry voice, "Steven, how many times do I have to tell you to put the milk back in the refrigerator?!"

This **event** in Steven's life triggers a lot of conscious and unconscious **thoughts,** such as:

"Here she goes, on my case again."

"She has no right to yell at me!"

"She is always mad about something."

"I'm tired of her putting me down all the time."

These thoughts produce a **feeling** of anger and resentment, which then trigger the following **actions:**

A scowl

A stiffening of the back

... and the following sharp reply:

"Why are you always making such a big deal out of everything?!"

This behavior triggers Steven's mother to respond with an angry remark of her own:

"Well, I wouldn't have to make a big deal out of it if you'd show a little responsibility!"

Mom's autocratic style and her punishing remark continue to trigger Steven's rebellious attitude and thinking:

"She can't treat me this way!" shouts and storms out in anger.

... and the cycle continues.

The Failure Cycle

When a child reacts to events in his life with low self-esteem and a poorly developed system of values, the discouragement and negative behavior that follow usually produce more negative events, such as failure and punishment. In Steven's case, these events might include getting into more power struggles with his mother or even causing problems at school or with peers.

Such misbehavior often provokes harsh criticism and punishment from autocratic adults. For the child, this triggers more faulty thinking and lower self-esteem, more discouragement, and more negative behavior and failure. Before long, a cycle of frustration and failure can develop. A child who has gotten caught in a failure cycle will need a lot of support and encouragement to break out.

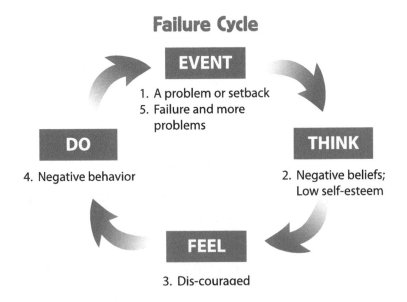

Failure Cycle

EVENT
1. A problem or setback
5. Failure and more problems

THINK
2. Negative beliefs; Low self-esteem

FEEL
3. Dis-couraged

DO
4. Negative behavior

The Success Cycle

A child with a well-developed set of values and high self-esteem might have responded very differently to his mother's criticism. He may have **thought:**

"Whoops, I messed up."

"Mom's pretty angry about the milk."

"I wish she wouldn't get so upset about it, though."

"Maybe I can help calm her down some."

These thoughts produce **feelings** of genuine remorse and courage, which then trigger the following **actions:**

A concerned look

Eye contact with Mom

... and the following positive reply:

"My bad. Here, let me put it back."

This positive behavior triggers Mom to respond with a softer remark:

"Okay, but remember on your own next time, please."

This becomes a new **event** for the child's Think-Feel-Do Cycle, and he responds with:

"Sure, Mom. I'll make a point to remember."

When a child has high self-esteem that is based on positive values and behavior, he can take a mistake, or even a failure, and turn it into a positive experience — one in which he learns from his mistakes. This positive behavior usually produces additional successful events, including positive feedback from adults. These successes strengthen self-esteem and courage, motivating the child to produce more effort and positive behavior and thus more success. This is what we call a *success cycle*, and it can be summed up by the popular expression "nothing succeeds like success."

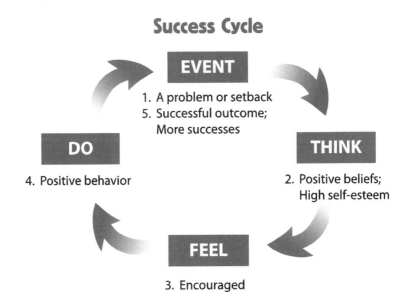

Success Cycle

EVENT
1. A problem or setback
5. Successful outcome;
   More successes

DO
4. Positive behavior

THINK
2. Positive beliefs;
   High self-esteem

FEEL
3. Encouraged

The Flooding Response

Sometimes a child becomes so frustrated that the feeling part of the brain releases chemicals that flood the thinking part of the brain, and a meltdown of sorts occurs. You know it as a tantrum. During such times the child temporarily loses the ability to use the higher-level, rational part of the brain and reverts to the more primitive parts to control behavior. Trying to talk rationally to a child during one of these episodes is about as useful as trying to stop an actual flash flood with a lecture.

Some children — often referred to as "spirited" children — experience a more extreme version of this flooding response. When they become overwhelmed, it's not your typical twenty-minute tantrum. Their epic tantrums can last a couple of hours or until someone helps the child calm down and regain his equilibrium. In Chapter 5, we'll be addressing ways that you can help children learn to manage anger and calm down when they become flooded.

What can parents do?

Helping our children get into success cycles and stay there is a goal for all parents. Helping them develop the character necessary to be successful within the rules and limits of society is a responsibility of all parents. Helping them to build faith and a strong relationship with God is a responsibility of all Christian parents. It is therefore important for us to become skilled at encouraging the development of self-esteem, courage, and character. But what does that word "encourage" really mean?

Breaking the word into two parts, *en-courage* means "instill courage."

en*courage*

"instill courage"

Rudolf Dreikurs once said, "Children need encouragement like plants need water."

Rudolf Dreikurs once said, "Children need encouragement like plants need water." Encouragement is the fertilizer that nourishes our children's courage, self-esteem, character, and skills. Wherever it is applied, we see more growth. Do you want your child to be a good reader? Encourage her reading. Do you want him to be honest? Encourage acts of honesty. What about responsibility, cooperation, courage and faith? Where you sprinkle encouragement, you spur growth.

The word "encourage" is mentioned over 100 times in the New Testament. Encouragement from parents and mentors, friends and teachers, and other believers is how many of us originally became Christians, and it is vital to our own children's spiritual growth. 1 Thessalonians 5:11 (NIV) entreats us: "Therefore encourage one another and build each other up, just as in fact you are doing."

The remainder of this chapter will be devoted to strengthening your encouragement skills so that you can help your child develop the character traits she needs to thrive.

The Power of Encouragement

> "Encourage one another daily, as long as it is called Today."
>
> *Hebrews 3:13 (NIV)*

Imagine yourself in this situation:

You are driving home in your car. Suddenly, in your rearview mirror you see a police car with blue lights flashing, and it is following you. Anxiously, you pull over, wondering what you did wrong. You notice your rapid heartbeat, the perspiration forming on your palms, your dry mouth. The policeman approaches your car window and asks for your driver's license. He looks at the license, then at you, and says, "You know, I've been on the force for 12 years, and it's always a pleasure to see a courteous driver. I pulled you over so I could congratulate you on the fine driving skill you showed back there in that traffic tangle at the freeway overpass. If every driver were as considerate as you, we could avoid lots of snarls and headaches. So I just wanted to say, 'Thanks.'"

What do you think your reactions would be to the policeman's comment?

    a. You would feel good about yourself, and a little proud.

    b. You would feel that you are a pretty good driver.

    c. You would feel encouraged to drive more courteously and considerately in the future.

    d. You'd almost faint from the shock!

Chances are that "d" would be your strongest reaction. We just do not expect to receive such compliments from authority figures. And yet, after the shock has worn off, you probably would feel good about yourself, think that you are a pretty good driver, and feel encouraged to drive more courteously and considerately in the future.

This is an example of the power of encouragement. With only a few words, the policeman increased your self-esteem, gave a boost to your confidence, and created the likelihood that you would drive even better in the future. No wonder some call encouragement "the subtle giant."

Our children soak up what we say, so we must seek to use words that are sprinkled with God's grace and avoid those that undermine it.

Unfortunately, in every opportunity to **encourage** our children (as well as ourselves and others) there is also an opportunity to **discourage** them. Which way we go depends on the words and actions we use. Our children soak up what we say, so we must seek to use words that are sprinkled with God's grace and avoid those that undermine it. Ephesians 4:29 (NIV) elaborates: "Do not let any unwholesome talk come out of your mouths, but only what is helpful for building others up according to their needs, that it may benefit those who listen."

In the New Testament, we learn the story of Saul, a man who made a career of violently persecuting early Christians. But one day a remarkable experience changed all of that. Acts 9:3-6 (NIV) tells us: "As he neared Damascus on his journey, suddenly a light from heaven flashed around him. He fell to the ground and heard a voice say to him, 'Saul, Saul, why do you persecute me?' 'Who are you, Lord?' Saul asked. 'I am Jesus, whom you are persecuting,' he replied. 'Now get up and go into the city, and you will be told what you must do.' " This was the beginning of a new life for Saul. He converted to Christianity and was given a new name, Paul. Following his conversion, Paul becomes one of the greatest encouragers ever known to the Christian faith.

When Paul mentored the early followers of Christ, he didn't *demand* that they spread the Word of God; rather, he encouraged each of them to develop a personal style of witnessing. He built on their existing strengths, he showed confidence that they could succeed, and he valued the spiritual gifts that each of them had to offer. Paul writes in 2 Timothy 1:7 (NIV): "For God has not given us a spirit of timidity, but of power and love and discipline." It is possible that we would not be Christians today had Paul not turned from his former life as Saul, aggressively discouraging the first followers of Christ, to a new life dedicated to building Christianity and writing words of encouragement that have endured through the ages and inspired generations of believers.

We all need an important person in our lives who believes in us and encourages us to be our best selves. For Paul, that was Barnabas. He convinced others to listen to what Paul had to say. Without Barnabas's support and encouragement, Paul may never have risen to the great deeds for which he would become known. As parents, we must strive to be that important person for our children. Our encouragement will help them develop their God-given skills and talents, just as Paul did for his followers, and just as Barnabas did for Paul.

Our encouragement will help them develop their God-given skills and talents, just as Paul did for his followers, and just as Barnabas did for Paul.

Because most of us are not natural-born encouragers, we need to work at recognizing our own discouraging tendencies while strengthening our ability to encourage. Before we look further at encouragement, let's consider its opposite — discouragement — and the ways it affects children's behavior.

Turning Discouragement into Encouragement

The misbehaving child is usually a discouraged child. Somewhere along the line, she lost the courage to face life's problems with positive behavior. Because negative behavior is easier and does not come with the risk of failure, she comes to believe that it is the only path open to her.

Referring again to the Think-Feel-Do Cycle: when a parent says or does something that discourages a child (Event), it tends to lower the child's self-esteem (Think), which leads to discouragement (Feel), which leads to negative behavior (Do). This may prompt the parent to become even more punishing and discouraging, and the cycle spirals downward. To avoid this pattern, we must do our best to stop discouraging our children and instead become encouraging events in their Think-Feel-Do Cycles.

The misbehaving child is usually a discouraged child. Somewhere along the line, she lost the courage to face life's problems with positive behavior.

First we need to be able to recognize when and how we might be discouraging our children. Although abuse and neglect are the most serious forms of discouragement, we are going to focus our attention on four less obvious but extremely common ways that parents can discourage their children and how each of these can be turned into a method of encouragement.

Discouraging Events	Encouraging Events
Overprotection and pampering	Stimulating independence
Focusing on mistakes	Building on strengths
Expecting too little	Showing confidence
Expecting too much (perfectionism)	Valuing the child as-is

Stimulating Independence vs. Overprotecting and Pampering

Independence is essential for thriving in our modern society. In fact, when we keep our children overly dependent on us, not only do they pay a price, but so do we. As psychologist Haim Ginott wrote, "Dependence breeds hostility." Overprotecting and pampering does not lead to the appreciation that parents may expect. It leads to resentment. Anything that keeps our children overly dependent on us works against our job as parents: to work ourselves out of a job.

Avoid pampering your child. When parents put themselves into their child's service or otherwise treat the child like a privileged character, the child eventually becomes dependent, spoiled, and discouraged.

Avoid overprotecting your child. When parents tell their child that the world is too dangerous and difficult for her, and they try to protect the child from both danger and failure by handling things for her, the child may come to believe that she is incapable of handling things for herself. Since she never learns to solve her own problems, she does not get the opportunity to make mistakes, experience their consequences, and learn from them.

Some signs of pampering and overprotecting a child include: calling her more than once to get up in the morning; routinely driving her places on short notice; picking out her clothes; giving her money on demand instead of an allowance; allowing her to curse and speak disrespectfully to you; not monitoring media (TV, music, movies, Internet, etc.); making her homework your responsibility; often letting her eat meals in front of the TV; always cleaning up after her; not requiring her to help with family chores; and saying things like:

> *"Sure, I'll be glad to talk to your teacher. I'm sure when she realizes how hard you worked, she'll change your grade."*

> *"I shouldn't have to call you three times to get up in the morning, but at least you're getting to school on time."*

In short, if you are doing things for your child on a regular basis that she could do for herself, if you often rescue her from the consequences of her misbehavior, you are pampering and overprotecting your child. It's time to

stop. Let her know you are going to start treating her more respectfully. You can do this in a firm yet friendly way, taking responsibility yourself while still encouraging your child:

> *"Forgive me for treating you like you don't have the good sense to get yourself up in the morning;. From now on I'm going to stop treating you like a baby and leave it up to you."*

"I don't use that kind of language when I'm angry with you; I don't expect you to use it when you're angry with me."

"I'll be glad to show you where dirty clothes go, but from now on I'm only washing the clothes that get put there."

Help your child develop a sense of interdependence. Life in our diverse, modern society is neither independent nor dependent. It is *inter*dependent. We are all traveling in the same boat, and learning to work cooperatively with others is a key to success, for both the individual and humankind as a whole. You can invite cooperative behavior from your child, with the aim of letting her experience the pleasure and benefits of group efforts.

"You're an important part of this family, and we'd like your ideas at family meetings."

"Why don't you come up on the sofa and snuggle with us?"

"Would you like to make lasagna with us?"

God highly values interdependence in our families and in the communities beyond our homes. Scripture teaches us:

> **"For as in one body we have many members,
> and not all the members have the same function,
> so we, who are many, are one body in Christ,
> and individually we are members one of another.
> We have gifts that differ according to
> the grace given to us."**

Romans 12:4-6a (NRSV)

Allow natural consequences to teach. In Chapter 3 we learned that natural consequences can be great teachers. They can be particularly effective for teaching independence. But don't forget that natural consequences are not always a good choice for discipline. See page 111 to review "When You Can't Use Natural Consequences to Teach."

Allowances and Chores

Giving children an allowance to spend how they choose stimulates their independence by teaching them responsibility with money. Plus, it provides a great response to the age-old question every parent hates to hear: "Can I have_____ ?" (As in, "Can I have that doll, game, candy bar, whatever I just saw advertised on TV," etc.) You can simply respond, "That's what your allowance is for."

The flip side of allowances is chores. Requiring your children to do a fair share of household chores encourages them to become both more interdependent and more responsible. Everyone likes to contribute to the well being of his or her family, even those who don't know it yet. It increases their feelings of significance and belonging, builds skills, and boosts self-esteem.

Chores and allowances go together well. Together they teach kids that, "All of us share in the work of running this family," and that, "All of us share the resources of this family." Here are some tips to make allowances and chores more effective:

- **Pick an allowance amount based on your child's age.** We recommend that you start giving weekly allowances when your child is around age 6 or 7. This is when children typically begin developing the ability to think abstractly, which is necessary in order to grasp the concept of money. Select the amount based on what you expect the allowance to cover (see the next point), and plan to increase it annually.

- **Determine what allowance will cover.** With young kids, just tell them that this is their money to spend however they would like. Let them know that you will still pay for all their regular needs, but that allowance is for extra things they may want but don't need. As they get older, discuss what allowance should cover in more detail, increasing the amount to cover things like entertainment, meals out without parents, and extra clothing. This may be a good time to discuss tithing and other options for children to put aside a portion of their allowance to contribute to their church.

- **Do not tell them how to spend their money, except in matters of health, safety, and family values.** Otherwise, let the natural consequences of spending money unwisely do the teaching. Better to learn now with small, kid-sized purchases than later, when they might spend a fortune on an overpriced _____ (fill in the blank from your own personal experience, because we have all had them!).

■ **Do not pay kids to do chores.** It can be tempting to do this, but it's better to keep allowances and chores separated. If your child wants to earn extra money, you can "hire" him to do jobs for you personally, like shining shoes or washing your car, *in addition to* his regular chores.

■ **Use discipline skills as necessary.** Rather than giving allowance as a reward for completing chores (or withholding allowance as punishment for forgetting chores), you can use the discipline skills you learned in Chapter 3 to help kids remember to do their chores. Here's one related logical consequence that effectively combines chores and allowances: If a child forgets to do his chore by the agreed-upon time, anyone else in the family can do it for him, and the child who forgot must pay the other person an agreed upon amount. This is logical because adults also have to pay others to do our work if we choose not to do it ourselves.

■ **Let kids participate in choosing chores.** Rather than dictating chores to your children, hold a family meeting to let them decide for themselves. Encourage them to choose chores they can reasonably do. Make sure someone writes all of this down.

■ **Rotate chores from time to time.** Children will be less resistant to accepting the less-pleasant chores if they know they will only have to do it for a short time. If they think they will be stuck taking out the garbage and changing the kitty litter forever, they may grow up to write parenting books.

■ **Teach your child how to do a chore the way you expect it to be done.** Don't assume that your child knows how to do something because you know how to do it. This could be a perfect opportunity to use the BANK Method described later in this chapter. You'll find more helpful guidelines in the "Teaching Skills" family enrichment activity in Chapter 5. Above all, keep it encouraging!

■ **Encourage saving.** Give your child a piggy bank or help her open a savings account. Then sit down and talk about the importance of saving money for more expensive things, rather than blowing it all on impulse purchases. You can encourage this further by offering to contribute a percentage of her savings towards a worthwhile goal.

■ **Encourage giving some to charity.** Help your kids use some of their own money to give to charitable causes. You may want to have a family meeting about giving and then plan what they want to contribute and to where. They will feel better about giving if it is their own choice and if they get to pick the cause they support. Again, be sure to encourage their giving for the generosity it is.

Building on Strengths vs. Focusing on Mistakes

If somebody important to you spends a lot of time telling you what you do wrong, you come to believe there is more wrong with you than right. If that important person yells or sounds disgusted with you, it hurts even more. If he calls you names or attacks your character, you may begin to believe that you are as bad as he says you are. Ironically, it becomes harder to do things right because you're so worried about making mistakes and causing further disappointment.

Maybe you have worked hard to correct a problem or improve your behavior and all she notices is what is still not right. You feel that your effort has not been appreciated, and wonder why you should bother to try again in the future. You lose motivation and your performance drops further, which prompts more discouraging comments until finally you feel like a certified loser.

A key to building successful behavior, is to focus the majority of your feedback on what your kids are doing right

This is how a child feels when his parent constantly points out his mistakes and seems to see only his weaknesses. The ways parents do this might be subtler than you expect. For example:

"I notice you left your glass in the den again last night. How many times do I have to ask you to be more considerate?"

"This doesn't look good where you colored outside the lines, does it?"

"Did you notice how easily your man beat you down court for that basket? You've really got to hustle back on defense."

The BANK Method of Encouragement

Kids do need to know what mistakes they have made in order to learn from the experience and do better in the future. We are not suggesting that you never mention these things. The error many parents make is to point out the mistakes and misbehavior but ignore the successes and positive behavior. A key to building successful behavior, however, is to focus the majority of your feedback on what your kids are doing

Focusing your attention on what's right, rather than what is wrong, is tremendously encouraging to the child.

right. This builds their confidence and motivates them to want to keep improving. In fact, if you and your child are locked in a power struggle or revenge cycle and you want to break out, find something about the child that you like. Focusing your attention on what's right, rather than what is wrong, is tremendously encouraging to the child. And, as we've seen, encouragement leads to improved self-esteem, which leads to courage and positive behavior ... in other words, a success cycle.

To help you remember how to use this important aspect of encouragement effectively, keep in mind these four letters:

Baby Steps

Acknowledge

Nudge

Keep encouraging!

Just as a bank is a place where resources are invested for growth, you can use the BANK method to help your child build her personal assets and grow into a successful human being. Let's look at the four letters one by one:

B for Baby steps. Break the learning down into baby steps. Remember, you didn't learn to walk all at once. You learned step by step. This learning process is the same for most things. Whether it is helping a child learn to complete his homework, or teaching him to be honest, we can break the task into steps and progress through them one by one. This makes the goal less daunting and allows the child to experience multiple successes along the way instead of just one at the end.

"I know school can be difficult, but if we break each assignment down into small steps you'll find that you can do it."

151

"If we want to teach Dani to be honest, let's take it day by day and encourage her every time she tells the truth when she could have lied to us."

A for Acknowledge what your child does well. Once you have identified a goal for your child (for example, having good study habits or being honest), get an idea where the child is on the path towards reaching that goal. It is unlikely that he can't read a single word. Acknowledge what he can already do well in order to build confidence and motivation to take the next step.

"You're already doing a great job of writing down your homework assignments. That will help a lot."

"I'm not thrilled that you borrowed my things without asking, but I do appreciate your owning up to it when I asked. I appreciate your honesty."

It is much more effective to "catch 'em being good" than our traditional approach of catching them being bad. It also helps to acknowledge other areas where the child is already experiencing some success. This helps build the self-esteem that translates into risk taking and other successes. For example:

"It was really a pleasure having you out to dinner with us tonight. Your manners were great. Let's do it again soon."

"Thank you for helping with the dishes."

"It sure is fun to play with you when you take turns with me."

N for Nudge the child to take the next step. Children get a sense of self-esteem from learning, whether they are learning a sport, a school subject, or a skill. As we have seen, learning requires many steps and gradual improvement. It also requires risk, because with each new step, there is the potential for failure. And there are times for all of us when the frustration of not progressing the way we'd like undermines our courage to persevere and tempts us to give up. This is when an encouraging nudge can help give the child enough courage to take the next baby step. For example:

"Long division can be frustrating. I guess you feel like giving up. But if you'll stick with it, I know you'll get it. Look how far you've come already! Now, how about tackling that last problem again?"

"I know it hasn't been easy, but you've really improved in being honest with us. And we're feeling like we can trust you more. So, if you still want to spend the night at Carrie's house, it's okay with us."

"You can do it. Go ahead."

"Let's take a break and then try again."

K for Keep encouraging improvement and effort. Arthur Blank, co-founder of the tremendously successful Home Depot and owner of the Atlanta Falcons pro football team once said that although he is a highly competitive person, he never sees the finish line. In other words, life is a process where success is measured in growth and improvement rather than any single end result. The mistake most parents make in the encouragement process is to wait until the child attains a desired goal before offering encouragement. One misguided father actually said that he was waiting for his son to graduate before complimenting him on his schoolwork!

Breaking the process down into baby steps opens up the opportunity for us to offer encouragement along the entire route. Any improvement, no matter how small, is a step in the right direction and should be noticed and acknowledged. Since success is a great motivator, we want the child to be able to experience numerous successes along the way. This builds self-esteem and keeps the child moving towards the goal. If the child falls back a step (and that's to be expected) she needs our encouragement to keep at it and not give up. In fact, her effort alone, even when she's not making progress, should always be encouraged.

Since success is a great motivator, we want the child to be able to experience numerous successes along the way. This builds self-esteem and keeps the child moving towards the goal.

"Great! You are really getting good at doing your homework at the same time every day. One more day and you'll have a whole week."

"Thanks for telling us about not turning in your homework on Monday. That took a lot of courage. We'll talk about what to do about it in a minute, but first I want you to know how much we admire your efforts to be more honest."

"I can really see the effort that went into this."

"I really like the way you stick with it."

Showing Confidence vs. Expecting too Little

When those we value most show confidence in our abilities, we tend to gain confidence in ourselves.

If people who are important to you don't believe in your ability, you probably won't believe in it either. They don't have to say so; you can usually tell what they think of you by the way they act around you and the words they use with you. People pick up on those things pretty easily. If someone never asks your opinion, you guess that they don't think you have much useful to say. If they seem satisfied with your half-hearted efforts at school, you figure they think that mediocrity is all you are capable of. If they do not encourage you to participate in a sport or other activity, you sense that they don't think you can handle it. Of course, sometimes they make their opinions crystal clear by saying such things as:

"No, you can't use that! You'll break it."

"I guess you're just not the type who does well in school."

How to Show Confidence

A cornerstone of self-esteem and courage is the belief that we are capable of success, whether in school, at work, with friends, family, or a love relationship. As we achieve success in solving life's problems and learning new skills, our belief in ourselves grows. But tackling problems and attempting new skills takes confidence. When those we value most show confidence in our abilities, we tend to gain confidence in ourselves.

There was a famous experiment in which teachers were told that results from an intelligence test showed that some of the students in their classes were highly intelligent and capable of excellent work while others were not. What the teachers did not know was that the results of the intelligence test had nothing to do with which students they were told were brighter. In fact, the students had been assigned at random. At the end of the year the students' grades were compared. Guess which group did better? As you might expect, the students in the so-called "intelligent" group had higher grades. The teacher's expectation that they were capable had made a significant difference in the students' ability to succeed. Such is the power of positive expectations on performance.

Giving your child responsibility is a nonverbal way of showing confidence. It is a way of saying, "I know you can do this."

Parents can also help their children succeed by showing confidence in them. Here are some ways to do this:

Give responsibility. Giving your child responsibility is a nonverbal way of showing confidence. It is a way of saying, "I know you can do this." Of course, you want to give responsibilities in line with what you know about your child's abilities, or the standards may be set too high. Here are some examples of giving responsibility in ways that demonstrate confidence:

> *"I will agree to your keeping the dog, Julie, if you will accept the responsibility of feeding and caring for her."*

> *"You've handled getting yourself up in the morning really well, so you can probably handle staying up later now — say, 9:00 p.m. What do you think?"*

Ask your child's opinion or advice. Children like to have parents lean on their knowledge or judgment. When you ask your child's opinion, you are demonstrating confidence in his ability to make a useful contribution. If you ask your child to teach you something, it shows confidence in his knowledge and skills. Asking for his opinions helps bolster his self-esteem:

> *"Which route do you think would be best on our trip to visit Grandma and Grandpa?"*

> *"What would you like to do with the toys that get left on the floor?"*

> *"Would you teach me to play your new video game?"*

> *"Well, what were the reasons for the Civil War?"*

Avoid the temptation to take over. It is an act of confidence in our children's abilities when we refuse to step in and take over when they become discouraged. What a temptation it is, this tendency to relieve their discomfort by doing the thing that is so hard for them and so easy for us! But when we give in to the temptation, we are not showing confidence in the child. If we do something for the child on a regular basis that she, with a little persistence, could do independently, then we are communicating a lack of confidence in her ability to follow a task through to the end. When we bail her out of the consequences of her misbehavior, we rob her of an important lesson in responsibility. We say, in effect, that we don't have confidence in her ability to handle the consequences of her actions.

All in all, taking over is not a way to encourage children who are discouraged; it is a way to certify their discouragement. Such children often show an inability to tolerate frustration. When things don't work out immediately, they give up, often having a "frustration tantrum" in which they are overwhelmed with anger and frustration at their inability to accomplish a task. Avoid this by encouraging your child to stick with the task with words such as these:

> *"Keep trying. You can do it!"*

> *"No, I can't stop the kids from teasing you, but I can talk to you about some things that you can do."*

Expect success and positive behavior. Like the teachers in the study who expected certain students to succeed, your expectations of your children are a powerful influence on their behavior. In fact,

Children often live up or down to our expectations.

So, why not expect them to succeed?

Children often live up or down to our expectations. So, why not expect them to succeed?

When you let them know that you think they can do it — whether "it" is doing well in school, being polite in social situations, following family rules and values, or anything else — you are encouraging them to live up to your expectations. They will sometimes mess up, and they will need your encouragement not to give up when this happens. And, of course, you need to keep your expectations in line with reality. After all, expecting a child to go from Cs and Ds to straight As overnight is setting you both up for failure. But expecting that your child can improve and using the BANK method to encourage his improvement is a recipe for success.

> *"I know you can improve your grades if you set your mind to it."*

> *"I'm counting on you to use your best manners at Grandma's house."*

> *"I expect you to tell me the truth."*

Valuing the Child As-Is vs. Expecting too Much

Positive expectations are important, but there is such a thing as expecting too much from your child. For example:

> *"How did you misspell 'circus' when you got all the others right? If you'd really thought about it, you would have had a perfect paper."*

> *"This isn't a bad report card. But with your potential, you could have done better."*

> *"You've got to practice, practice, practice until you play the piece perfectly. How else do you expect to be any good as a violinist?"*

If your parents expect more from you than you are able to give, you gradually stop trying because you know you will never be able to satisfy them. You may decide to make your mark in other ways, like misbehaving. Since you can't be the best at being the best, maybe you can be the best at being the worst. Or maybe you will become a perfectionist yourself in a futile attempt to please your parents and feel good about yourself. Life becomes one big worry as you try harder and harder. But even when you succeed, you cannot enjoy it for fear of what challenge to your self-esteem is coming next.

How to Value the Child As-Is

A child's self-esteem does not spring from achievements alone. It is much more important for most people to be accepted by significant people in their lives — to belong. In fact, much of our effort to be successful is really fueled by our desire to win the acceptance of those significant people. What most of us really want deep down inside is to be accepted for being ourselves, not for our achievements.

What most of us really want deep down inside is to be accepted for being ourselves, not for our achievements.

The baseball pitcher Tim Wakefield was once asked before pitching the biggest game of his young career if he was nervous. His answer was no, because, he reasoned, no matter what happened that night, the next day three things would still be true: his parents would still love him, his friends would still love him, and God would still love him. Armed with that core acceptance for who he was, his success in life, as measured by personal satisfaction, was well on its way.

Children who feel accepted by their parents have a bedrock of self-esteem upon which to construct a healthy, happy life. Without it, some of the wealthiest, most accomplished people in history have lived lives of quiet desperation, wondering why their successes were never satisfying.

The goal for parents is to communicate to our children that win or lose, pass or fail, in the limelight or in the line-up, we are still their parents and we are glad of it. We all need this unconditional acceptance from someone, and if we don't get it from our parents, we need to get it someplace else: from a substitute parent, or even a therapist.

The goal for parents is to communicate to our children that win or lose, pass or fail, in the limelight or in the line-up, we are still their parents and we are glad of it.

Separate worth from accomplishments. A child's worth is less a matter of what he does, and more a matter of who he is. You can let your child know that while you admire his successes and share disappointment in his failures, you love him for himself. Emphasize the importance of participation in the activities themselves and not just on the results. Encourage your child while he is doing a task instead of waiting until the task is completed.

> *"I'm glad you enjoy learning new things."*

> *"Playing your hardest is more important than winning."*

> *"Losing doesn't make a person a loser."*

Separate worth from misbehavior. Just as a child's worth is not the sum total of her accomplishments, it is also not the sum of her misbehaviors. A useful way to approach this is with the attitude that there are no bad children, only bad behavior. If a child is labeled "bad" or "no good," she may eventually come to believe that about herself, and then bad behavior will feel appropriate to her. After all, what should we expect from "bad" people but "bad" behavior? This self-fulfilling prophecy makes it vitally important that we refrain from labeling or shaming children for their mistakes or misbehavior. Children who grow up ashamed of themselves have a difficult time regaining their lost self-esteem and courage.

Mistakes, like misbehavior, are not indications of a lack of worth, but are actually part of growth and development. A mistake can teach a valuable lesson, showing a child what not to do in the future. We want to help children, especially perfectionists, learn to make friends with their mistakes and not to be ashamed of them.

Children (and adults) who are afraid and ashamed of making mistakes actually block their own growth and development. A perfectionist, according to one joke, is a person who won't attempt a foreign language until he can speak it fluently. A fear of mistakes yields a fear of trying, which in turn yields less learning. Since one of our goals is to help our children learn, we want to help them accept mistakes with a smile, rather than a kick.

> *"No, you're not bad, but coloring on the walls is not okay. Let's find a good place to color."*

> *"When we get angry at you, it doesn't mean we don't like you. It means we don't like something you've done."*

> *"Mistakes are for learning. When we make a mistake, we don't blame. We correct it."*

> *"I guess you made a mistake. Well, let's see what you can learn from it."*

Appreciate the child's uniqueness. Although it is important to teach children that all people are equal, that doesn't mean all people are the same. It is encouraging for your child to know that she is unique, special, one of a kind. You can appreciate your child's uniqueness by taking an interest in her activities. Most of all, you can say and do things that show your child you love her for her unique self, and for no other reason.

> *"Anyway, that's my opinion. What's yours?"*

> *"I love your sense of humor. Nobody can tell a joke like you!"*

> *"You are the only you in the whole world. What luck that you happen to be my daughter!"*

> *"I love you."*

Encouraging our children is not always easy, especially when we are overworked and overwhelmed. Yet God's Spirit within can give us the power, the love, and the discipline we need to be the encouraging presence our families need. Romans 12:1-2 (MSG) teaches us where to begin:

> So here's what I want you to do, God helping you: Take your everyday, ordinary life — your sleeping, eating, going-to-work, and walking-around life — and place it before God as an offering. Embracing what God does for you is the best thing you can do for him. Don't become so well-adjusted to your culture that you fit into it without even thinking. Instead, fix your attention on God. You'll be changed from the inside out. Readily recognize what he wants from you, and quickly respond to it. Unlike the culture around you, always dragging you down to its level of immaturity, God brings the best out of you, develops well-formed maturity in you.

Family Enrichment Activity: Letter of Encouragement

Many years ago as a young Sunday school teacher, Michael Popkin discovered a powerful method of encouragement. At the end of the school year he decided to write each of his students a letter about the progress they had made during the year. As he wrote the letters, he found himself focusing only on the students' strengths and what he liked about them. The students politely accepted these "letters of encouragement," as we now call them, as they left for summer vacation.

Michael didn't think much more about these letters until four years later. He was at a reception when a woman approached him and introduced herself as the mother of one of his students from that Sunday school class. "That letter you wrote Alice," she said, "meant so much to her. You know, she still has it pinned on her bulletin board."

What Michael learned from that experience is that "putting it in writing" carries extra weight in our society, and that this is as true with encouragement as it is with anything else. In addition, when you write a letter of encouragement, your child can refer to it in the future and rekindle the warm feelings it generated, just as Alice did.

The Apostle Paul, great encourager that he was, understood the power of the written word when he wrote The Epistles, which now make up many books of the New Testament. Make no mistake: these letters to the Romans, Corinthians, Galatians, and many other early followers of Christ were letters of encouragement. They have never lost their power. In fact, they still inspire and encourage Christians today.

This chapter's family enrichment activity is to write your child a letter of encouragement. In future weeks, you may also want to experiment with "texts of encouragement," e-mails, even brief videos, but right now try a throw-back to good old fashioned letter writing.

Keep these tips in mind as you do:

- Write about improvements, not necessarily accomplishments.

- Be specific.

- Write only truthful comments. Don't say your child has improved when he hasn't.

- Write what you appreciate or enjoy about your child.

- Include how your child's behavior has helped others.

- Emphasize God's presence in your child's life.

Dear Ben,

Your mother and I have been noticing how well you are doing with your reading. We can really hear the improvement. All your hard work is paying off! Pretty soon you will be able to read anything you want to all by yourself.

I am also proud of the way you are taking responsibility for your schoolwork. You are getting your homework done every school night like we talked about. You are also giving it your best and not rushing just to get it done. Your teacher seems to have noticed the improvement also. That must make you feel good.

Thanks also for helping me clean up the garage the other day. You have grown to where you are a big help around here! Plus, you have always been great company with your sense of humor and positive attitude.

Ben, God made you unique and special. There is no one else exactly like you! God is always there for you and wants only the best for you, just as your mom and I do. You are a gift from God and a blessing in our lives. And if I forget to say it often enough, I'm real glad that you're my son.

Love,

Dad

Family Meeting: Character Talks

Building positive values and character in our children is a matter of using many of the skills in this book — from discouraging behavior that reflects negative values with the discipline skills in Chapter 3 to encouraging behavior that reflects positive ones. We can do this in little ways throughout our everyday interactions with our children and through the examples we set through our own words and actions. But the notion that "values are caught, not taught" is only partly true. Group discussion can also be an effective way to encourage positive values.

This chapter's family meeting is to discuss an aspect of character with your family. This is what we call a *character talk*. It will help you understand and influence your child's developing beliefs and values that underlie the development of character. Topics can include anything that will contribute to a person's character. (See the list on page 167 for some ideas.)

Character Talk Guidelines

The following tips will help you get your first talk off to a good start.

1. **Plan how you will introduce the topic, and write down points you want to cover.** Starting a group discussion is often the most difficult part. It is helpful to plan how you will introduce the subject. Topics for future talks might be chosen by different family members, and each might prepare his own introduction. Be sure to list important points you want to make during the meeting so you don't forget them. A simple introduction for your first talk might go something like this:

   > *"We called this meeting because we want to take time now and then to talk about topics that are important to all of us — topics that have to do with the kind of people we are becoming. And I say "we" because parents are still growing and changing too. The topic I've chosen for our first talk is courage. Let's begin with a prayer."*

2. **Ask open-ended questions to stimulate discussion.** Once you have introduced the topic, having a few good questions ready can help

launch the discussion. Prepare these ahead of time and make sure that they are open-ended. This means that they cannot be answered with a simple "yes" or "no."

Closed Questions	Open-Ended Questions
"Do you think courage is important?"	"What are some ways that courage is important?"
"Is fear always bad?"	"When do you think fear might be a good thing?"
	"When can giving in to fear get you in trouble?"
	"What does courage mean? Is it just physical courage, or are there other types of courage?"
	"What is an example of a time when you had to choose between courage and fear?" (Be ready to share an example.)

3. **Listen with empathy as you discuss the topic together.** Remember to use your Active Communication skills from Chapter 2 and listen with empathy to your child's thoughts and feelings. This will help develop his own emotional intelligence and encourage him to continue sharing. Avoid communication blocks as you keep an open, nonjudgmental attitude about his thoughts and feelings. Be careful when he says something that goes against your own value system not to judge or criticize (even nonverbally with a negative facial expression). If you do, you run the risk of shutting him down and you limit your chance to influence his thinking about this.

"That's an interesting point. I hadn't thought of courage being used like that."

"You must have been frightened when that happened, and yet you didn't quit."

"I'm not sure I agree with you about that, but it does give me another way to look at it."

4. **Share your own values persuasively.** Children today are less likely to automatically accept our values and beliefs just because we tell them. Being a positive influence requires accurate information, sound reasoning, and persuasive arguments. Bringing in outside resources such as a relevant online video, an article, a movie, book, or even a TV show can help lend weight to your point of view. Sometimes relating a personal experience can create a story in your child's mind that helps her learn an important lesson. The more relevant you can make your examples to your child's experience, the better chance you have of getting through to her core beliefs and values.

"I thought the Natalie character in that movie showed a lot of courage in standing up to her friends who wanted her to cheat on the exam."

"When we don't try because we are afraid we'll fail, we don't even have a chance to succeed. Remember, you get some of what you go for, but you don't get any of what you don't go for. And remember that God is always with us and loves us no matter the outcome."

"To this day, I still have regrets about not trying out for the basketball team."

"Remember the courageous people in the Bible."

Topics for Character Talks

Courage is only one of many possible topics for a character talk. You might also consider having a talk about one of these topics or others that you and your family feel are important:

Cooperation	Hard work
Honesty	Perseverance
Respect	"Paying it forward"
Self-esteem	Patriotism
Giving to charity	Healthy habits
Helping victims of bullies	Volunteering
Being a friend	Compassion

"Fruits of the Spirit" (Galatians 5:22-23)

As you apply your encouragement skills in your family this week and hereafter, draw strength from these powerful words from Scripture. You might remember them from Chapter 2, but they are worth repeating here.

"May our Lord Jesus Christ himself and God our Father, who loved us and by his grace gave us eternal encouragement and good hope, encourage your hearts and strengthen you in every good deed and word."

2 Thessalonians 2:16-17 (NIV)

5: Understanding & Redirecting Misbehavior

▸ *Judy was worried about her five-year-old son, Nathan. Although he had been in kindergarten for most of a year, he did not seem to have any friends. He often seemed sad and had occasional outbursts of anger. Then one day she saw him in the yard cutting a worm in half, and her alarm bells went off. She had heard that cruelty to animals was a warning sign that a child was seriously troubled, so she consulted a neighbor who had six children of her own and was therefore an "expert" on parenting.*

The neighbor confirmed that Nathan's behavior was indeed the sign of a serious problem. Furthermore, she warned Judy, without immediate psychiatric intervention, Nathan might end up beyond anyone's help. "And then who knows what we'd have on our hands?" she remarked meaningfully. Judy knew how to read between the lines. She rushed home in tears, arriving just in time to greet Nathan's carpool.

When the carpool driver asked to speak to her privately, Judy expected the worst. Once inside, the carpool mother shared her concern. "I hope you won't be offended by this, but I overheard Nathan telling my daughter, Taylor, about cutting a worm in half yesterday." Judy's heart skipped a beat as she prepared for the bomb to drop. "She asked him why" the carpool mom continued, "and he said … well … so the worm would have a friend to play with."

Hearing these words, Judy finally understood the message her son had been sending through his behavior. He wasn't an antisocial criminal-to-be after all. He was a sensitive, shy boy who was lonely.

"So, I was thinking," continued Taylor's mom, "that maybe we could arrange some play dates between Nathan and Taylor. What do you think?"

"I think that's a great idea," answered Judy with a sigh of relief.

> **"Give me understanding, so that I may keep your law and obey it with all my heart."**
>
> *Psalm 119:41 (NIV)*

Understanding children is never easy. All parents wonder and worry to some extent about why their children do what they do and how they are going to turn out in the long run. This is especially true when it comes to unusual behavior or outright misbehavior. The point of the opening story about Judy and Nathan is not to dismiss the idea that some children have special needs that should be identified and treated as early as possible. The point is that behavior is complex and we cannot always know what is behind a child's behavior or misbehavior by just observing. After all, when you were a child, didn't your parents ever indicate their frustration with something you did by saying such things as:

"I just don't understand you!"

"Why do you do things like that?"

"What were you thinking?!"

Talking to God can bring understanding to the most confusing of subjects. You need only to ask.

The truth is that you probably did not know why you did what you did, and your children don't either. So asking them is not going to help. Asking God, on the other hand, is always a good idea. Don't forget that. God did not leave us to figure out parenting on our own. Isaiah 41:10 (NIV) reassures us: "So do not fear, for I am with you; do not be dismayed, for I am your God. I will strengthen you and help you; I will uphold you with my righteous right hand." Talking to God can bring understanding to the most confusing of subjects. You need only to ask.

The purpose of this chapter is to show you a way of better understanding how and why your children behave as they do.

We will then combine that understanding with the CAP methods we have been learning. This will help you to redirect your children towards positive behavior when they misbehave or just need some guidance. We'll begin with some basic information about child development.

Nature vs. Nurture

A newborn baby is small, helpless, and absolutely dependent on someone else for her own survival. Someone else must feed, clothe, cuddle, and comfort the infant. She cannot survive alone, much less thrive. How does such a helpless creature develop into an independent adult with a personality of her own? There have been many theories about this, but two of them continue to influence current thinking:

The Nature Theory: The basis of the "nature" theory is that hereditary factors, genetically transmitted from parent to child, play the major role in forming a child's personality. This view holds that a child's development depends entirely upon the biological package with which he is born, that genes alone determine all physical, mental, and emotional factors and mold the personality into its unique shape. When a child misbehaves, according to this theory, it is due to the influence of "nature."

The Nurture Theory: According to the "nurture" theory, environmental influences such as the child's home, school, neighborhood, parents, nurturing, and other circumstances play the dominant role in shaping the personality. With this view, one could conclude that a child is like a lump of clay, whose development is shaped by outside influences, and his unique personality is the result. When a child misbehaves, according to this theory, it is because of how his environment has "nurtured" him.

Today, most experts believe that the credit for who we become should be split about 50/50 between genes and environment (or between "nature" and "nurture"). But this does not tell the whole story either.

An Active Theory: There is another school of thought that holds that while heredity and environment are important influences on development, it is the way the child uses these influences that matters most. In this view, the child is not a passive victim of heredity or circumstance; rather, he is an active participant in his own development, building a unique personality by the way he responds to whatever influences come along. The child's destiny is not left entirely to fate. It is also a matter of choice. We are ultimately each responsible for who we are and what we do. In other words,

> ### It's not what we have that is important.
> ### It's what we do with what we have.

After all, history is filled with examples of individuals who overcame difficult challenges to lead satisfying lives and become contributing members of their communities.

This does not mean that heredity and environment do not influence our personality and behavior. Sometimes circumstances are so overwhelming, as in the case of war or natural disaster, that they can overwhelm a child's ability to choose. Circumstances such as abuse, poverty, and lack of access to education and healthcare can also stack the deck against a child's ability to succeed.

A Look at the Building Blocks of Personality

We might think of all of the positive and negative influences that individuals use to shape their lives as their "building blocks." Since a child with better building blocks is more likely to survive and thrive, it is useful to consider some of these influences more closely.

Among the most important of our building blocks are heredity, family atmosphere, family constellation, and methods of parenting.

Heredity

The biological package — or the set of genes — that a child inherits from her parents is an important resource that she can use to build a personality. This includes obvious traits such as eye color, hair type, height, body type, and other aspects of appearance. But it also includes aptitude for various skills such as art, music, sports, math, science, and language. Of course, whether the child fully develops these aptitudes depends on environmental factors (for example, whether the child's family can afford guitar lessons or whether the schools she attends have good math teachers) and how hard the child chooses to work. The same is true of intelligence. It is likely that nature gives us each a range of intellectual functioning, and where she winds up in that range depends on how she is stimulated by her environment and how she applies herself. Finally, it seems that genes also give the child her temperament. Some children are naturally more spirited

(and challenging to parents!) than others. Some are more compliant. Some are outgoing while others tend to be introverted. But the temperament that nature provides is only a starting point. The child shapes and changes her temperament as she responds to her environment and makes choices. For example, a child with a spirited temperament can grow up to be a bully and then a violent criminal, or she can learn to channel her spirited nature positively and become a successful leader. Which direction the child goes depends on a combination of outside influences such as parenting and her own choices.

Some children are born with special needs that become building blocks in their own right. These can create both challenges and opportunities for the child — and for the entire family. How the family (as well as the school and community) responds to these needs will influence how the child uses the needs as building blocks. Does she get the help she needs to thrive in spite of limitations? Does she learn to build on her strengths or does she gain more by using her needs to put others in her service? Does she strive to thrive or is she happy just to survive?

For a young child, the family is the world. Almost all of a child's early influences come from the family.

Family Atmosphere

For a young child, the family is the world. Almost all of a child's early influences come from the family. The atmosphere of the family's home is therefore very important. What does it feel like to live in the home? Is there a feeling of mutual respect and cooperation? Are the parents warm and caring? Is there good humor? Time for fun? Are girls and boys treated with equal love and respect? For Christians, faith and how it is observed is a major contributor to the family atmosphere.

Whatever atmosphere prevails, the child will respond to it, and that response becomes a building block of his personality. Children's responses can take many forms: optimism, pessimism, rebelliousness, obedience, shyness, confidence, or anything in-between. The possibilities are endless.

Family Constellation

Another influence on a child is the number of other children in her family and the order of birth. No two children come into exactly the same family. For example, a firstborn child comes into a family of two adults (or sometimes only one). The second child enters a family of adults and a sibling. The child's position in the family influences the role he will play in that family and in the world in general.

Research has shown that as a group, first children are likely to have certain characteristics in common, as are youngest children, middle children, etc. The chart on the next page shows some of these common characteristics and some ways parents can avoid magnifying their negative aspects. In using the chart, keep in mind that when more than a five-year gap exists between any two children, the effect is as if there were two separate families. For example:

Lisa (16) is treated as if she is an only child; Jason (9) is treated like a first child; and Susan (7) is treated like a second child.

Family constellation is an important building block for children. But understand that it is not so much the child's position in the family as it is his *view* of the position that makes a difference in the way he develops. You and your children may or may not fit these typical characteristics, depending on decisions you have made.

Methods of Parenting

The building block over which parents have the most control is their style of parenting. Let's review the three styles or methods that we discussed in Chapter 1:

1. **Autocratic Style (The Dictator):** The Dictator parent is an all-powerful figure who uses reward and punishment as tools for keeping everyone in line. Children are told what, how, where, and when to do most things. There is very little room for them to question, challenge, or learn to make their own decisions.

2. **Permissive Style (The Doormat):** The Doormat parent allows the children too much freedom. There are few limits placed on

Family Constellation Chart

	More likely to...	To help, parents can...
FIRST CHILD	take responsibility for other siblings get along well with authority figures become a high achiever be a perfectionist feel superior to others	avoid pressuring him to succeed emphasize the value of participating, not just winning teach that "mistakes are for learning" show how to accept mistakes with a smile, not a kick
ONLY CHILD	be the center of attention be unsure of herself feel less competent than others (e.g. parents) be responsible refuse to cooperate unless she gets her way	provide learning opportunities with other children encourage visiting friends have overnight company use childcare and nursery schools
SECOND CHILD	try to catch up with sibling's abilities try to be sibling's opposite rebel in order to find his own place	encourage his uniqueness avoid comparisons with sibling allow him to handle sibling himself, or in family meeting
MIDDLE CHILD	feel left out, unsure of position be sensitive, bitter, or vengeful be a good diplomat or mediator be spoiled by parents and siblings	make time for one-on-one activities include her in activities and discussions ask for her opinion
YOUNGEST CHILD	be treated like a baby be self-indulgent be highly creative be clever	not rescue him from every conflict refer to him as "the youngest," not "the baby" encourage self-reliance not regularly do for him what he can do for himself

children and little respect for order and routine. Many permissive parents behave as doormats, allowing their children to walk all over them. In such a system, children experience insecurity because there is no feeling of cooperation or belonging, and children are left wondering, "Who is in charge here?"

3. **Authoritative Style (The Active Parent):** Active Parenting is, in some respects, a balance between the autocratic and permissive methods, but it is much more. In an Active Parenting household, parents and children have rights and responsibilities. The parent is the leader who encourages cooperation and stimulates learning. There is order and routine, freedom within limits, and every person in the family is an important member.

When it comes to parenting our children, we want to give them the best building blocks we can. This does not guarantee that they will "survive and thrive in the kind of society in which they live," but it will greatly improve their chances.

Understanding Behavior: Purpose, Not Cause

We've established that children's behavior is influenced by outside events such as the style with which a child is parented and how encouraging or discouraging the parents are. But we have also learned that these events do not directly *cause* the child's behavior. Human beings have free will. We choose how to behave based on our experience, values, and goals for the future. So to understand why your child behaves the way she does, ask yourself:

- *What is the purpose or goal of their behavior?*

- *What payoff is their behavior aimed at getting?*

A person's goals influence his behavior, but since this occurs at an unconscious level, it is often difficult to know what motivates someone.

For example, on what seems like a typical school morning in the Chandler household, 5-year-old Nicholas refuses to put on the shirt that his mother has picked out for him. Mom yells and threatens, begs and bargains, but Nicholas simply will not put on that shirt. Why is he refusing to comply with his mother? What is his purpose or goal? Does his behavior get him the payoff he wants? To answer these questions, let's look at four basic goals of all children's behavior, and then see which one Nicholas might achieve through his behavior.

Four Goals of Child Behavior

In Chapter 1 you learned that the purpose of parenting is to protect and prepare our children to survive and to thrive in the kind of society in which they will live. Building on the foundation laid by Rudolf Dreikurs, Active Parenting recognizes four goals that humans consider essential for surviving and thriving. These same four goals motivate the majority of our children's behavior:

belonging

power

protection

withdrawal

Let's look at each of these goals more closely.

Belonging

To belong is a basic need of every human being. A baby could not survive without others to depend upon. Neither could the human species have survived throughout history without belonging to various groups: clans, families, communities, city-states, kingdoms, and nations, to name a few.

To belong is a basic need of every human being.

This desire to belong motivates each of us to make contact — physical or emotional — with other human beings. For an infant, the need to be held is actually critical to its wellbeing. Later, contact with Mom and Dad helps the growing child develop a sense of belonging in the family. The self-esteem and courage that grow out of this sense of belonging make it possible for the child to form positive relationships outside the family. Schools, religious organizations, sports leagues, and other institutions offer additional opportunities for contact and belonging.

Power

Each one of us wants to influence our environment and gain at least a measure of control over our lives. We would like for things to go our way, and we want the power to make that happen. It is through learning that we become able to do this. As the saying goes, "Knowledge is power." As parents, we want to empower our children to develop their talents and skills and become competent individuals who contribute to the common good.

Protection

To survive and thrive we must be able to protect ourselves, our families, and the society in which we live. The human instinct to repel both physical and psychological attacks has led us to develop complex systems of justice and defense. Children will also look for ways to protect themselves from physical harm or from threats to their self-esteem. But because they lack a mature understanding of justice and the interconnectedness of people, they often strike out in ways that are unproductive and even harmful. Parents and teachers can help children learn responsible methods of protection while providing a safe environment in which they can develop.

Withdrawal

Just as a child seeks contact with others, at other times he needs to withdraw and regroup. Withdrawal is a kind of counterbalancing act to the goal of belonging. Our early survival instinct has also taught us to withdraw from danger. We can teach our children that taking time alone with God for meditation and prayer is a helpful and healing form of withdrawal.

Positive and Negative Approaches to the Four Goals

There are no good or bad children, only children who choose to pursue these four basic goals in either positive or negative ways.

An interesting aspect of these four basic goals is that they may be approached through either positive or negative behavior. The CAP approach stresses that there are no good or bad children, only children who choose to pursue these four basic goals in either positive or negative ways. Children with high self-esteem and courage will generally choose positive approaches. Those with low self-esteem, who are discouraged, are more likely to choose a negative approach. This is one reason why it is so important to learn to become active encouragers of children.

The following chart shows the positive and negative approaches that children take to the four goals:

Negative Approach	Child's Goal	Positive Approach
Undue attention-seeking	**Belonging**	Contributing, cooperating
Rebellion	**Power**	Independence, competence, assertiveness
Revenge	**Protection**	Assertiveness, justice, forgiveness
Undue avoidance	**Withdrawal**	Appropriate avoidance

The Parent-Child Cycle

Often we act as if other people have the ability to control our feelings:

"You're making me angry."

"You make me happy."

No one can make us think, feel, or do anything without our permission.

The truth is that we are responsible for our own strong emotions, and assuming that responsibility is empowering. No one can make us think, feel, or do anything without our permission. Why give that power to someone else? As the expression goes, "When we feel, we deal." And we have the perfect partner in God to stand alongside us in the "dealing" process.

Although other people and events do influence or *trigger* our feelings, the actual cause of our feelings is usually found in our own beliefs, attitudes, and values — in other words, what we think. This is also where the four basic goals of behavior operate. We can show this more clearly by mapping it onto the Think-Feel-Do Cycle:

The Think-Feel-Do Cycle and The Four Goals

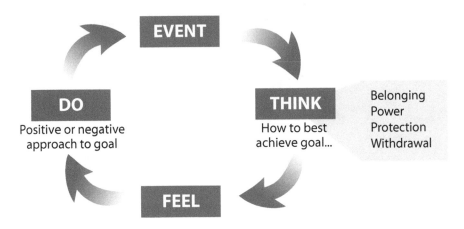

During the "Think" step of the cycle, the child chooses a goal (though this is usually a unconscious process) and considers how to best achieve it. This produces a feeling. Together, the thinking and feeling, much of which is also usually unconscious, produce a behavior — either a positive or negative approach to the goal.

When a parent is involved in the interaction, the parent's behavior is often the event that triggers the child's Think-Feel-Do Cycle. Likewise, the child's response to the parent is often the event that triggers the parent's Think-Feel-Do Cycle. We can diagram a parent-child interaction by combining the two cycles like this:

The Parent-Child Cycle

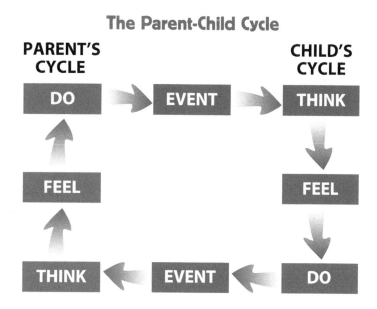

Unless one side does the unexpected and changes the interaction, the cycle will continue or even escalate until parent and child physically separate.

Unless one side does the unexpected and changes the interaction, the cycle will continue or even escalate until parent and child physically separate ... and then resume later with a new triggering event.

To illustrate how the Parent-Child Cycle works, let's look at an example of a child at the dinner table, pursuing the goal of belonging through the negative approach of undue attention seeking. Looking at the chart on the next page, start with number one under "Think" on the child's side. Then follow the numbers around the cycle to see how the interaction takes shape between the child and the parent, ending at number 15.

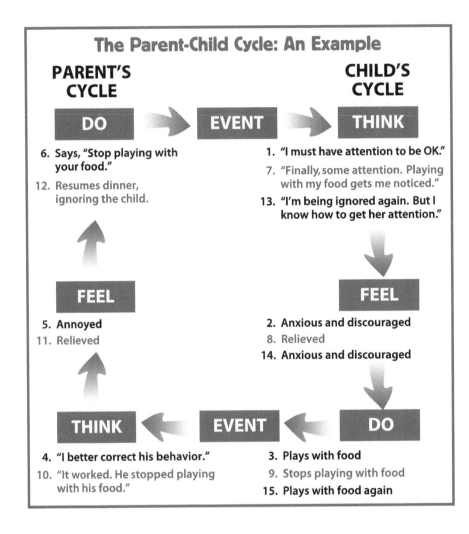

The Parent-Child Cycle: An Example

PARENT'S CYCLE

CHILD'S CYCLE

DO → **EVENT** → **THINK**

6. Says, "Stop playing with your food."

12. Resumes dinner, ignoring the child.

1. "I must have attention to be OK."

7. "Finally, some attention. Playing with my food gets me noticed."

13. "I'm being ignored again. But I know how to get her attention."

FEEL

5. Annoyed

11. Relieved

FEEL

2. Anxious and discouraged

8. Relieved

14. Anxious and discouraged

THINK ← **EVENT** ← **DO**

4. "I better correct his behavior."

10. "It worked. He stopped playing with his food."

3. Plays with food

9. Stops playing with food

15. Plays with food again

What can the parent do to avoid paying off the misbehavior and break the cycle? Did you notice how the mother actually paid off the child's negative approach by giving him the undue attention he wanted? In the case of undue attention seeking, we want to act more and talk less. The discipline that works best is either a brief confrontation through an "I" message or a logical consequence. For example:

"Either stop playing with your food or you will need to leave the table. You decide."

This logical consequence does give the child some brief attention. However, if the child resumes playing with his food, the parent then follows through with the consequence. For example:

> *"I see you have decided to leave the table tonight. Please put your plate in the sink and we will try again tomorrow."*

Now, the child must deal with the consequence of getting no attention at all, which spoils his pay-off and breaks the cycle. Remember, however, that kids will test to see if we will be consistent with our new approach, so this parent should expect more undue attention seeking behaviors in other areas, at least for a while.

Note: If the child refuses to leave the table, she is moving into the negative approach of rebellion. We'll cover this negative approach next.

Remember that discipline is only half of the process for redirecting misbehavior. Discipline is designed to limit the negative behavior. However it is just as important to actively encourage the child toward the positive approach. In the case of undue attention seeking, we want to help the child achieve the recognition and contact he wants by playing a useful role. In the above example, the mother may have involved her son in the conversation by asking him a question. We can help find meaningful ways for a child to contribute to the family while ignoring some of the unproductive attention-getting behaviors. Using the encouragement skills you learned in Chapter 4 will help.

Determining Your Child's Goal

Because parents do not usually know the goals behind a child's misbehavior, we often take an action that makes the problem worse. In other words, our discipline actually pays off the child's negative behavior by helping her achieve her goal. And if negative behavior works, why not continue to use it? After all, it's usually the easier approach.

The first step, then, is to determine what your child really wants. Once you know the goal, you can help redirect the child to choose a positive approach to getting it. This requires some detective work on your part. There are two clues that will usually tell you a child's goal:

1. **Your own feeling during a conflict.** Are you annoyed, angry, hurt, or helpless? Because much of a child's misbehavior is aimed at the parent, becoming aware of your own feelings during a conflict can be a powerful clue to the child's goals.

2. **The child's response to your attempts at correcting the misbehavior.** How does your child behave after you have made an effort to correct the misbehavior?

The following chart is a guide for interpreting the answers to these two questions:

If you feel...	And your child's response to correction is to...	Then the negative approach is...	To your child's goal of...
Annoyed	Stop the behavior, but start again very soon	Undue attention-seeking	Belonging
Angry	Increase the misbehavior or give in only to fight again another day	Rebellion	Power
Hurt	Continue to hurt us or increase the misbehavior	Revenge	Protection
Helpless	Become passive; refuse to try	Undue avoidance	Withdrawal

Redirecting Your Child's Behavior

Remember the shepherd's rod we talked about in Chapter 3? Just as shepherds of old used a rod to guide their flocks, modern-day parents use a symbolic "rod of discipline" to guide their children. Shepherds also used their rod to redirect wayward sheep back to the fold. Parents' symbolic rods of discipline serve this purpose, too. It's part of our job as parents to keep our children from wandering into danger. So when we see a child starting down a path of misbehavior by choosing the negative approach to reach their goal, we need to guide the child back to the positive approach.

The key to helping your child shift from a negative to a positive approach with any of the four goals is to do the unexpected. You have to break the pattern the child has come to expect, avoiding the payoffs that maintain their mistaken ideas.

Do the unexpected. You have to break the pattern the child has come to expect, avoiding the payoffs that maintain their mistaken ideas.

Keep in mind that a misbehaving child is usually a discouraged child. Each of the four negative approaches of misbehavior represents an increasing level of discouragement, from undue attention seeking to avoidance. If your child is into revenge or avoidance, it could take considerable time and effort, perhaps even outside help, to redirect him to the level of encouragement where he is in a success cycle. Be patient; use your CAP skills, and keep encouraging him. Now, let's look more closely at each of the four negative approaches.

A Child's Solution

Dr. Popkin once heard from a mother whose four-year old would fly into a terrible tantrum when he didn't get his way. Finally the mother, trying to engage her son in some problem solving, asked what she could do to help prevent these meltdowns. The child replied without the slightest bit of irony, "Just do what I want."

Negative Approach 1: Undue Attention-Seeking (Goal: Belonging)

The child who seeks belonging through undue attention-seeking probably has the mistaken belief that she must be the center of attention in order to belong. Such children find ways to keep people busy with them. An undue attention-seeking child may act forgetful,

or helpless, or lazy, putting the parent in his service with reminders and coaxing. Or the child may get attention by clowning, asking constant questions, pestering, or making a nuisance of himself. He may even resort to positive behavior, but only if there is a parent to watch. When the parent hears, "Look at this, Mommy," over and over again, even positive behavior can be for the wrong purpose.

Adults typically feel annoyed or irritated during these interactions. When we correct the child, he will usually stop the misbehavior. After all, our correction has given the attention the child seeks. However, the child will usually want more contact soon, and will resume the misbehavior.

How parents pay off the negative approach of undue attention-seeking: We tend to remind, nag, coax, complain, give mini-lectures, scold, and otherwise stay in contact with the child. This attention is the payoff that reinforces the child's mistaken approach to achieving contact. To such children, even negative attention is better than no attention.

What can you do to avoid paying it off?

- Act more and talk less.

- When you must discipline, briefly confront your child with an "I" message or a logical consequence.

- Help your child achieve the recognition and contact she wants by playing a useful role. Help find meaningful ways for her to contribute to the family while ignoring some of her unproductive attention-getting behavior.

- Teach her how to play alone by introducing hobbies and other activities.

Negative Approach 2: Rebellion (Goal: Power)

The ability to say "no" is very powerful ... as every two-year-old quickly learns.

Of the four negative approaches, rebellion is the most common and creates the most distress in families and schools. The child who becomes discouraged trying to achieve his goal of power in a positive way can easily find power in the negative approach of rebellion. He does this by trying to boss others around or by showing them that they can't boss him. After all, the ability to say "no" is very powerful ... as every two-year-old quickly learns. In fact, one of the rules of power is this:

The person in a position to say "no" is in the more powerful position.

This is why power struggles are so frustrating for parents. We are bigger, smarter, more experienced, and have the authority to decide what's in the best interest of our families — but even so, we cannot make our children do what we want. They have the free will to choose, and if they choose to resist us, our frustration can easily turn to anger. This feeling of anger is a major clue that you are in a power struggle and that your child has chosen a rebellious approach to his goal of power. The other clue is that power-driven children are very persistent and often respond to correction by continuing the misbehavior, often in open defiance. For example: "No! You can't make me!" We'll cover anger and power struggles in more depth later in this chapter.

How parents pay off the negative approach of rebellion:

Parents who tend towards the Doormat style often make the mistake of giving in to rebellious children. These parents want to avoid confrontation and so give in to the child's unreasonable demands and refusals. The pay-off is that the child gets her own way. "Look how powerful I am. I made Daddy give in!"

Parents who tend towards the Dictator style often fight fire with fire. Words such as, "No, you can't make me!" are fighting words to an autocratic parent. It hooks their own desire for power by triggering thoughts such as, "I've got to be in control here; I'm the parent!" and of course, "Oh yes I can!" They meet the child's challenge with a show of force and wind up fighting, either verbally or with punishment. Ironically, the more you fight with a child over power, the more she perceives that she is winning. After all, even if she eventually does what you want, say after a spanking or other punishment, she still has the secondary payoff of knowing that she made you angry. This in itself is very powerful. "Look how powerful my rebellion makes me. I made Daddy so mad!"

> *Ironically, the more you fight with a child over power, the more she perceives that she is winning.*

What can you do to avoid paying it off?

- Refuse to fight or give in, and sidestep the struggle for power.

- Give choices instead of orders. Express confidence in your child's ability to make decisions for herself.

- Take your sail out of your child's wind. In other words, call a "time out" and excuse yourself until you both calm down.

- Let her make mistakes and experience the consequences without lecturing or humiliating her.

- Hold family meetings to involve your child in making decisions that affect the whole family.

- Use family enrichment activities, communication skills, and encouragement to build a more cooperative relationship.

- Use the FLAC method (described later in this chapter) to defuse the power struggle and set consequences only when necessary.

- Set a good example of how to use anger positively.

Negative Approach 3: Revenge (Goal: Protection)

Revenge is one of the oldest and most primitive motivations for human behavior. It is also one of the most counterproductive. It grows out of the goal of protection. "You hurt me. If I hurt you back,

Revenge is one of the oldest and most primitive motivations for human behavior. It is also one of the most counterproductive.

you'll think twice before hurting me again," seems to be the thinking that produces this behavior. And because revenge does often work as a deterrent, children and adults alike continue to use it. The problem is that revenge usually leads to more revenge in an ever-escalating cycle of hurt and retaliation.

This escalation can be seen in the violence of our society. People often take revenge (for either real or imagined injustices) through acts of violence. While kids with high self-esteem and courage are able to pursue their goals of protection through assertiveness (standing up for themselves), justice (using legal channels to address their grievances), and forgiveness (clearing the slate so that neither side feels the need to retaliate), those with lower self-esteem and more discouragement often resort to revenge.

Within a family, we often see how an escalation in a power struggle can easily lead to the negative approach of revenge, especially if the child feels that the parent has "won too many battles," or has hurt the

child in the process. The child decides that the best form of protection is to hurt back. And while this seldom results in physical violence, the child still has ways to hurt the parent. In fact, it is this feeling of hurt that is the clue that the child is pursuing revenge. And because our autocratic parenting tradition tells us that when children hurt us we should punish them more, an escalating revenge cycle begins.

Because parents want to see their children survive and thrive, they can never win this revenge war. All children have to do to hurt parents is fail. They can fail at school; they can fail with peers; they can fail with drugs, with sex, and, ultimately, they can fail at life. The result each time is a parent left hurting.

How parents pay off the negative approach of revenge:

When children seek to protect themselves by getting revenge, they are usually feeling very discouraged. When we retaliate with punishment and put-downs, we discourage them further and confirm their belief that they have a right to hurt us back. The more we hurt them, the more they want to hurt us back.

What can you do to avoid paying it off?

- Stop the revenge cycle. Instead of stubbornly demanding that your child change, call a cease-fire.

- Remember that no child is born "bad" or "mean." When a child acts in a bad or mean way, she is hurting inside. Do what you can to stop whatever is hurting the child. If it's your behavior, take a new approach. If someone else is hurting her, support her while she handles it herself, or take more direct action if needed.

- Sometimes a vengeful child is hurting because he has a misconception about how life ought to work. This is the notion of a "perceived injustice," rather than a real one. Talk with your child about fairness and help him learn to see things from different perspectives.

- The FLAC method and other skills for handling a power struggle can also be useful in redirecting a revenge-seeking child.

- Work on strengthening your relationship with family enrichment activities, active communication, encouragement, and other support skills.

Negative Approach 4: Undue Avoidance (Goal: Withdrawal)

Children who become extremely discouraged may sink so low in their own self-esteem that they give up trying. Their belief becomes "I can't succeed so I'll stop trying, and then I can't fail." They develop an apathy that often leaves parents and educators feeling helpless.

Sometimes they adopt an "I don't care" attitude that shields them from the pain of losing, but also prevents them from growing and thriving. Such children may become truant from school, fail to do assignments, and avoid peers. In the teen years, tobacco, alcohol, and other drugs may become a way for them to avoid the challenges of life as they find temporary relief from their own discouragement.

How parents pay off the negative approach of undue avoidance:
It is sometimes our own perfectionism that contributes to the child's long, slow slide into undue avoidance. When we focus excessively on mistakes, when nothing ever seems to be good enough for us,

when all we talk about is his great "potential," the child may give up trying altogether. For other children it may be a special need or challenge that makes success more difficult. Without the support and encouragement of caring adults, they may fall further and further behind and become so discouraged they give up.

Once a child has chosen avoidance, we might make the mistake of giving up on him, write him off as "hopeless," and stop making an effort to help. Or we yell and scream, humiliate and punish. Either way, we send the message: "You're not good enough." This confirms the child's own evaluation of himself and justifies his avoidance.

What can you do to avoid paying it off!

- Communicate to your child that succeed or fail, win or lose, you are glad that she is your child. Your love is unconditional.

- Practice patience and offer a lot of encouragement. Use the BANK method to build on the child's strengths.

- Help your child find tasks at which she can succeed, which will help her gain confidence and improve her self-image.

- Help your child see that mistakes are for learning and that failure is just a lesson on the road to success.

Basic Goal of Child's Action	Child's Positive or Negative Approach to Goal	Child's Typical Beliefs	Parent's Typical Feeling	Child's Response to Correction	How to Redirect
Belonging	Contributing Cooperation	My contributions are recognized. I belong by cooperating. I enjoy human contact.			Encourage cooperation. Acknowledge the child's contributions.
	Undue Attention-Seeking	I belong only when I'm served or noticed. The world must revolve around me.	Annoyance	Stops, but begins again very soon	Ignore the behavior. Give the child full attention at other times. Use logical and natural consequences. Act, don't talk.
Power	Independence Assertiveness Competence	I am able to influence what happens to me. I am responsible for my life.			Allow increasing amounts of freedom. Continue to encourage.
	Rebellion	I belong only when I'm the boss or when I'm showing you that you can't boss me.	Anger	Escalates behavior or gives in only to fight again another day	Remove yourself from the conflict. Talk about it after cooling off. Don't fight or give in. Use FLAC method.
Protection	Assertiveness Justice Forgiveness	I can stand up for myself and those I love. I can forgive and even contribute to those who have wronged me.			Express positive feelings. Be assertive and forgive in your own relationships.
	Revenge	I've been hurt and will get even by hurting back. Then maybe they'll learn they can't get away with hurting me.	Hurt	Continues to hurt, or escalate misbehavior	Refuse to be hurt. Withdraw from the conflict. Show love to vengeful child. Avoid temptation to hurt back. Use FLAC method.
Withdrawal	Appropriate avoidance	There are times when I need to be alone. And there are situations to be left alone.			Respect wishes to be alone (only in safe situations). Don't press. Later, use Active Communication.
	Avoidance	I'm a failure at everything. Leave me alone. Expect nothing from me.	Helplessness	Becomes passive; refuses to try; gives up	Be patient. Find ways to encourage. Build skills using baby steps.

■ Get him extra help if he needs it, including professional evaluation and counseling, if you think necessary.

The chart on the preceding page provides an overview of the four goals of children's behavior, how and why they approach these goals, and some of the best roles for parents in each set of circumstances.

Avoiding Power Struggles

We discussed how the goal of power can be approached through rebellion, often leading to angry power struggles between parent and child. We also said that the secret to avoiding a power struggle is to neither fight nor give in. This, however, is not an easy task, but with a little parent "judo" it can be accomplished.

The goal is to make the problem the enemy and not the child. Remember, as soon as you get angry, you've lost the power struggle.

While Dictator parents tend to fight head on with a challenging child, judo is the art of sidestepping the opponent's attack and using his own thrust to throw him off balance. By not fighting or giving in to your child during a power struggle, but instead doing the unexpected, you can influence your child to change some of the thinking that drives this misguided approach to power. Unsurprisingly, there are an unlimited number of ways that you can "do the unexpected." But what they all have in common is that they require that you stay calm and friendly, and do not take your child's rebellion personally. The goal is to make the problem the enemy and not the child. (See the section on anger at the end of this chapter.) Remember, as soon as you get angry, you've lost the power struggle.

Here are some ways you can use your CAP skills to "do the unexpected" and avoid (or stop) a power struggle with your child:

■ Show confidence in your child's ability to make decisions by himself.

■ Rather than boss, give choices.

■ Let your child make some mistakes, and then experience the consequences ... without lecturing or humiliating.

■ Set up family meetings to involve your child in making decisions that affect the whole family.

■ Use the family enrichment activities, communication skills, and methods of encouragement described in this book to begin winning a more cooperative relationship.

And, most important,

■ Show your child that you are not interested in fighting. Instead, show him that you will work together to find solutions, and that when discipline is necessary, you will use logical consequences, rather than anger and punishment.

If you tend toward the Doormat style, you can also try these:

■ Refuse to give in to your child's unreasonable demands.

■ Stop being your child's short-order cook, clean-up service, wake-up caller, and last-minute chauffeur.

■ Set firm limits, negotiate within those limits, refuse to be intimidated by displays of anger, and enforce the consequences of breaking the limits.

■ Let your child know that while you believe she should be treated respectfully, you expect to be treated respectfully, too.

Now we'll see how a number of CAP skills can be combined to reduce the "flack" experienced in a power struggle.

The FLAC Method

The acronym FLAC can help you remember how to defuse a power struggle without fighting or giving in. The letters stand for:

Feelings

Limits

Alternatives

Consequences

Here's a situation we can use as an example. Nine-year-old Justin is angry about having to go to bed and keeps getting up for one thing after another. His father is about to get very angry, but then he remembers that getting angry and shouting at Justin is what his son expects and will only fuel the power struggle between them. Instead, he does the unexpected. He sits down on his son's bed and says:

(F for Feelings) *Father:* *I guess I really don't blame you for wanting to stay up later, Justin. I never liked going to bed, either. It feels like you're missing out on something.*

Justin: *(Surprised at his father's empathy) Yeah.*

(L for Limits) *Father:* *Still, we all need our sleep to stay healthy and function well the next day, so you can't just stay up until you crash.*

Justin: *But I don't want to go to bed now. It's too early.*

(A for Alternative) *Father:* *Hmm, well maybe there's an alternative. I might be willing to let you stay up an extra half hour if you were to use it as quiet time to relax yourself. Say, maybe by reading in bed.*

Justin: *Can I read fun stuff or does it have to be a schoolbook?*

(C for Consequences) *Father:* *You can read fun stuff. But here's the deal. If you are tired the next day or don't get up on time, or if you get out of bed after the half hour is up, then you have to go to bed on time the next night with no reading or hassle. Agreed?*

Justin: *OK.*

Let's review the four steps:

Feelings: We saw in Chapter 2 how important it is to listen and respond to our children's feelings. When we show empathy for their feelings about a situation, we suddenly move from being the enemy to being on their side in finding a solution to a common problem. This goes a long way towards defusing the power struggle ("don't fight") while laying the groundwork for a win-win solution.

Limits: By reminding his son of the limits of the situation and providing a good reason for the limits, Dad defines the problem to be solved ("don't give in"). It's much less provocative to say, "because the situation calls for this," rather than, "because I said so." In this case, the situation calls for a good night's sleep.

It's much less provocative to say, "because the situation calls for this," rather than, "because I said so."

Alternatives: Once people disengage from a struggle for power, you'd be surprised how often an acceptable alternative can be found. Losing thirty minutes of sleep is unlikely to cause a problem for Justin or his dad, and it has the additional benefit of encouraging the importance of reading. By negotiating within reasonable limits, we can often make the limits more palatable for our children. Even when the limits are firm, you can often find an alternative within those limits that makes it more acceptable to the child.

Consequences: Some writers suggest that consequences only make matters worse with a rebellious child. Others suggest coming down even harder in a display of "tough love." However, if you can avoid getting angry (which turns the logical consequence into a punishment) then consequences can be useful as one more tool in motivating the child to live within the limits. They do not need to be harsh, just firm enough to remind the child that he is responsible for his actions.

Parenting and Anger

> "My dear brothers and sisters, take note of this:
> Everyone should be quick to listen, slow to speak and slow
> to become angry, because human anger does not produce the
> righteousness that God desires."
>
> *James 1:19-20 (NIV)*

The management of anger has become recognized in recent years as vitally important to families and throughout society. Anger that turns to rage and then to violence creates headlines that range from school shootings and terrorist attacks to family violence. Even on smaller scales, children and adults who cannot control their tempers create pain for themselves and those around them. Yet anger is also a natural part of life, so what should we make of this complicated emotion?

Some of us may have had a parent who used anger to shame or manipulate. As adults, we often unintentionally repeat what we experienced as children, even the things that hurt us. Unless we learn a new way of dealing with our angry feelings, we could carry destructive anger from our past into our own families. When left unchecked, human anger, generation after generation, can wreak havoc on a family system.

To help our children survive and thrive, we must learn to deal proactively and positively with our angry emotions rather than denying, avoiding, or acting upon them.

One of the main reasons that CAP methods are effective is that they require parents to put aside anger when they interact with a child. The power of these grace-filled methods is born not out of anger but out of logical thinking and, even more important, love. To help our children survive and thrive, we must learn to deal proactively and positively with our angry emotions rather than denying, avoiding, or acting upon them. As Ephesians 4:26 (NIV) encourages: "In your anger do not sin: Do not let the sun go down while you are still angry."

The Purpose of Anger

Not all anger is bad. In fact, anger can be useful. Our ability to feel such a strong emotion is one of God's gifts to us. Anger is an emotional and physiological response to frustration. If an important need, want, or desire is blocked for us, our bodies and emotions react with intense feelings that we often label as anger.

For example, a caveman walking through the woods comes upon a fallen tree that blocks his path. On the other side of the tree are some berries he wants to pick and eat. He strains to push the fallen tree aside, but he isn't strong enough, and he becomes frustrated at the thought of not reaching his goal. His frustration produces changes in his body that enable him to lift the fallen tree and hurl it aside.

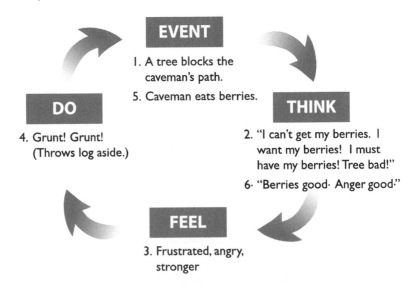

EVENT
1. A tree blocks the caveman's path.
5. Caveman eats berries.

THINK
2. "I can't get my berries. I want my berries! I must have my berries! Tree bad!"
6. "Berries good. Anger good."

FEEL
3. Frustrated, angry, stronger

DO
4. Grunt! Grunt! (Throws log aside.)

Anger is one of the emotions that triggers that ancient human instinct, the fight or flight response (see "A Little Bit about Your Child's Brain" on page 30 for a more detailed description). This causes our brains to release chemicals that make us stronger, faster, and ready to take action, whether it's to fight danger or run from it. In primitive times, this added power and focus helped us survive when problems could be settled by either being stronger or running faster than someone (or something) else.

Old Brain vs. New Brain

Anger originates in the more primitive "Emotional Brain" of young children. But over time, as the "Rational Brain" develops, so does human intelligence and the ability to make better decisions. As humans mature both as individuals and as societies, so does the ability to manage their emotions and handle problems with solutions other than brute force.

Using, not Losing, Your Temper

Even in modern societies, anger sometimes pays off. Rudolf Dreikurs observed that people do not lose their temper; they use their temper. What he meant was that people sometimes use anger to intimidate others into giving them what they want. Since anger is often accompanied by violence, this intimidation can sometimes be effective. But it carries a heavy price. Anger used to bully damages relationships and is hurtful. Worse yet, it can lead to violent behavior and crime.

The Message of Anger

Our own angry feelings tell us that one of our goals is being blocked. They clearly send this message:

"Act! Don't just sit there; get up and do something!"

If you do something soon, you can often solve the problem before it gets worse, and before you "blow up." If you don't act but try to ignore the message, several things could happen:

- The problem might go away by other means, but this is a risky and uncertain possibility.

- Your anger may grow in intensity until it propels you into action, which is likely to be desperate, unthinking, and potentially violent.

■ Your anger will fester internally, expressing itself in unexpected ways: headaches, rashes, ulcers — even heart attacks.

How to Use Anger Positively

Since anger is a natural response to frustration, and it can give us the motivation we need to do something about the event (or behavior) that is causing that frustration, our goal in handling anger is not to stop getting angry; rather, we need to learn to use our anger in positive ways and teach our kids to do the same. When you find yourself angry, the following four steps can help you use it, not lose it:

1. **First, acknowledge your anger early, when it is still small.** Don't wait for anger to get so intense that it overwhelms your thinking brain. Try to catch it early so that you can still take positive action.

2. **Next, hit the imaginary "pause" button in your Think-Feel-Do Cycle.** Imagine this button right before the "Do" step in your Think-Feel-Do Cycle. As soon as you notice yourself becoming angry and before you say or do something that you may regret later, hit that pause button and think about what is triggering your anger.

3. **If necessary, use self-calming techniques to reduce your anger.** Some people have a short fuse. In other words, the part of the brain that responds to threats with anger produces chemicals so quickly that they flood the rational brain before the brain knows what's happening. These people need to learn how to calm themselves down before they take action. If your child has a *spirited* temperament, then he probably needs help in this area. Some self-calming methods include:

   ■ Deep breathing

   ■ Taking a time-out (not as a punishment, but as a calming break)

   ■ Journaling or praying out your strong emotions

- Counting to 10 (or 20, or 100)

- Being held gently and talked to in low, calm tones

- Taking a warm bath

4. **Solve the problem or change your thinking about the problem.** This step requires your thinking brain, so either hit the pause button first or calm down before acting. Then use your anger to help you find a solution to the problem.

Handling Anger with Prayer

> "Get rid of all bitterness, rage and anger,
> brawling and slander, along with every form of malice.
> Be kind and compassionate to one another,
> forgiving each other just as in Christ God forgave you."
>
> *Ephesians 4:31-32 (NIV)*

It's natural to have strong negative emotions such as bitterness, rage, and anger from time to time, but we must not hold onto these feelings and allow them to smolder until we lose our temper and say or do things that could hurt feelings — or worse. We must learn to let go of our strong negative emotions. This is where prayer can really make a difference. We can "get rid of all bitterness, rage, and anger" during our quiet time with God.

As we discussed in Chapter 1, how you spend quiet time with God is a personal choice. Journaling your feelings to God can provide both cathartic relief and clear-minded perspective on your anger and other emotions. Going outdoors to take a walk while you talk with God can breathe fresh air into the situation. And using a method of prayer we call "palms-down/palms-up," described on the next page, is a powerful way to replace your negative emotions with the grace of God.

The "Palms-Down/Palms-Up" Way to Pray

Using the "palms-down/palms-up" approach to prayer can help you release strong or negative emotions so you can then be filled up with the power, perspective, and purpose of God. Here's how to do it:

Sit quietly in a comfortable chair or lie in bed. Place your palms down on your lap and empty before God all of the overwhelming emotions that have filled your mind and hurt your heart. Pour out every feeling and thought until nothing more is stirring inside you. Then turn your palms over. With your palms resting open and facing up, ask God to fill your emptiness with the gifts of the Holy Spirit:

> *"God, please fill me with Your power and Your peace."*

> *"Please give me Your loving perspective."*

> *"Please form in me the words that my child needs to hear."*

When you get up from your quiet time, you will be emptied of every form of malice and your strong emotions will be replaced by God's powerful presence.

Sometimes anger can come upon us suddenly and we do not have time to journal, take a walk, or enter into a long time of prayer. To get through these challenging situations, put off responding for a moment, take a deep breath, and silently pray for the Lord to intervene:

> *"God, please help me."*

> *"Please give me Your words, Lord."*

> *"Please take this burden of anger from me and replace it with your peace."*

These simple, silent prayers open your heart and mind to God and allow his power to work within you.

Helping Children Use Their Anger Positively

It is increasingly important in these days of "zero tolerance" for aggressive behavior that we teach children that violence is not an OK way to solve problems.

Because children are usually more primitive in their expression of emotions, they will often resemble a caveman when experiencing frustration and anger. Tantrums and hitting are fairly common with young children. However, it is increasingly important in these days of "zero tolerance" for aggressive behavior that we teach children that violence is not an OK way to solve problems. In addition to teaching them to use the four steps above to use their anger effectively, you can also do the following:

1. **Model good anger management.**

   The way you handle your own problems and frustrations will provide a model for your children. Ask yourself:

   - Do you fly into a rage, hurling insults and humiliation?

   - Do you strike out at others?

   - Do you sink into a depression?

2. **Help them find more effective forms of expression.**

   For example:

   "You have the right to feel the way you do, but in our family, we don't scream and blame; we look for solutions."

   "I can see that you are angry. Can you tell me with words instead of hitting?"

   "When you get angry at me, please tell me without calling me names. I don't call you names; please don't call me names."

3. **Remove yourself from a power struggle.** When children have tantrums, you can acknowledge their anger, but at the same time "take your sails out of their wind." Don't try to overpower the child; withdraw instead. This action says to the child, "I am not intimidated by your show of temper and will not give in, but I won't punish or humiliate you either." The result is that children who get neither a fight nor their own way after throwing tantrums will usually find more acceptable ways to influence people. If you need a quiet place to withdraw from the power struggle, try the bathroom. It's the one place where a little privacy is usually expected. For spirited children and other kids who have trouble calming themselves, stay with them and help them self-calm. Then work at teaching them self-calming methods later.

4. **Use the FLAC method.** In situations where a child's tantrum interferes with the rights of others (like in a restaurant, or when company is in the home), you can acknowledge the child's feeling, remind him of the limits, offer an alternative, and follow through with logical consequences. For example:

   "I know you are angry about having to go shopping with me, and I'll admit that it isn't much fun. Still, we do want to eat dinner tonight, so we need to get this done. How about you help me out by putting the food in the cart? That will make it go faster and then you can help me pick out some of your favorite desserts."

If the child continues to act out his anger, add a logical consequence:

   "Dennis, you can either calm down and help me shop or we will have to go sit in the car until you can. Then we definitely won't have time to stop by the park."

Children must learn that there are consequences for violent and aggressive behavior. The child who acts out his anger by breaking something can help pay for its replacement. The child who hits or bullies can be removed from other kids for a period of time to think about how he can make it up to the other person. As with all logical consequences, stay calm and firm when delivering them. Your goal is not to hurt the child — which may just begin a revenge cycle — but rather to teach him.

5. **Allow your child to influence your decisions.** When a person feels powerless to influence an authority, frustration gives way to anger and rebellion. If you allow your child to influence your decisions, she will not be as likely to resort to such unconscious tactics as bed wetting, soiling, and stomach disorders, to name a few.

The method your child uses to influence your decisions will be influenced by what you allow to work. If you "give in" to tantrums, whining, or tears, the child will learn to use these tactics again. If you redirect your child to express his anger respectfully, listen to his arguments, and sometimes change your decisions, then your child learns the important skill of negotiation.

Family Meeting: Problem Solving Using the FLAC Method

We've learned that as parents we need to teach our children to negotiate solutions to problems within limits that are acceptable for the situation. This can go a long way towards increasing harmony in families and preparing kids to succeed in our democratic society.

The FLAC method is an effective process for solving family problems as well as individual ones. Whether you have regularly scheduled family meetings or you call a meeting only when you need to solve a problem or end a power struggle, FLAC can help. Using the four skills in the FLAC method in a family meeting has the added value of communicating that:

We are a family of problem solvers.
Everyone's ideas and feelings are valuable.

The participation and respect generated can lessen power struggles while generating a cooperative energy that produces highly creative solutions to problems.

Before you use the FLAC method in a family meeting for the first time, you'll want to explain the method to your family by going over the steps. Do not feel that you have to follow these steps rigidly, but use them as guidelines to help your meetings run smoothly.

Problem-Solving with the FLAC Method

Step 1. Clarify the PROBLEM.

Step 2. Share FEELINGS and thoughts.

Step 3. State the LIMITS involved.

Step 4. Brainstorm ALTERNATIVES and choose one by consensus.

Step 5. Decide on CONSEQUENCES, if needed.

Step 1.   Clarify the PROBLEM.

It is important to begin by stating the problem in terms of behavior and not by attacking your child's personality.

Poor: *"I have a problem with you being lazy."*

Better: *"I have a problem with how messy your room is."*

Step 2.   Share FEELINGS and thoughts.

Remember that building our children's emotional intelligence means helping them learn to listen to other people's thoughts and feelings as well as their own. With that in mind, the next step is to encourage sharing. Use the skills we learned in Chapter 2 to avoid communication blocks while getting everyone's thoughts and feelings on the table.

Child:	*But it's my room, so what's the big deal?*
Mother:	*I understand it's your room, and that putting things away is a hassle. But I guess I've learned how important it is to be organized and I want you to be able to find things when you need them.*
Father:	*And I just feel kind of frustrated when I walk in there and clothes are laying everywhere, drawers half open, and toys all over the place.*
Child:	*Good, then don't go in there.*
Father:	*Well, I don't feel good about not helping you learn good habits.*

Step 3.   State the LIMITS involved.

Limits are sometimes set by outside authorities like governments, schools, or businesses, and reflect rules that everyone must live by (or help change). In the family, however, limits are often set by the parents as "family values." These values will vary from family to family. Many parents are OK with the child having a messy room as long as he keeps the mess from the public areas of the house. However, in the above example, these parents have a different value, and they are free to voice it.

Father:	*Besides, in our family we want to take pride in our home, and that means keeping it reasonably neat.*

Step 4.   Brainstorm ALTERNATIVES and choose one by consensus.

By generating possible solutions and discussing them as you go, you can often come up with something everybody can live with. This is called "consensus" decision-making. You don't vote, but rather continue to discuss until you find an agreement that everyone can accept. When a consensus cannot be reached, then it is up to the parents as leaders in the family to decide the best of the possible choices, taking into account everyone's thoughts and feelings.

> Mother: *Maybe we can think of a solution that everyone feels good about. Anybody have an idea?*

After discussion...

> Mother: *OK, then we agree that we won't bug you every day about cleaning your room, but you will take care of it before you go play outside on Saturdays. I'll help you organize it this Saturday so that you'll know what we expect from now on. Oh, and we all liked Dad's idea of taking a picture of it afterwards so you'll have a model of what it should look like before you have us come check it each week.*

Step 5.   Decide on CONSEQUENCES, if necessary.

In our example about the messy room, the family came up with a solution and logical consequence as part of their brainstorming in Step 4. However, there will be situations where a logical consequence is added after the solution is chosen in order to motivate the child to keep the agreement. Whether you need a consequence or not depends on your child's track record. If he has been responsible about keeping his agreements, then adding a logical consequence might be seen as disrespectful and may actually backfire. However, other kids with a history of testing the limits will usually understand the need to add a consequence.

Following Up

There is an old saying that "you get what you inspect, not what you expect." In other words, we need to expend the effort to make sure agreements are kept and that consequences are followed through. This also presents an opportunity to encourage a child for a good job, remind him of what still needs work, or provide further help, if necessary.

In the case of the messy room, if the child kept his agreement, it is essential that you encourage him with a word of praise or a positive "I" Message, as described in Chapter 3.

> Child: *OK ... I'm ready for somebody to check my room.*
>
> Father: *(looking around) OK...nice job. Let's just check the picture...very nice. Everything seems to be in place and I especially like the way you put your toy lion on the pillow. That's a creative touch. Your room really looks great.*

Of course, if there are still problems, you can compliment your child's progress and remind him about what still needs to be completed.

> Father: *Say, this is really starting to look good. I like the way you've organized things. Let's see ... the bed is made up in the picture but not here.*
>
> Child: *Oh, yeah ... I'll fix that.*
>
> Father: *Great. Make your bed, then you'll be all set to go outside and play.*

Family Enrichment Activity: Teaching Skills

Part of developing self-esteem and courage is seeing oneself as a capable individual. When you take the time to teach your child a skill, you not only help her become more capable, you also give her positive ways of achieving the goal of power. In fact, teaching your child a skill empowers her in a very positive way and enriches your relationship with her.

The following steps can help you teach a skill effectively:

1. **Motivate.** Encourage your child to want to learn the skill by explaining the value it has to the child or the entire family.

> *"You know how I'm always talking about how important it is to take care of your body by exercising and eating healthy foods, and how good you'll feel if you do? Well, how would you like to learn how to make something that's really healthy and really yummy, too?"*

2. **Select a good time.** Pick a time when neither you nor your child will be rushed or distracted by other activities.

3. **Break the skill down into baby steps.** You learned from the BANK method that there are benefits to breaking a skill down into smaller parts so that the child can learn it one step at a time. Not only does it make the task easier; it also allows the child to experience more successes, which helps build courage and motivation.

When you take the time to teach your child a skill, you not only help her become more capable, you also give her positive ways of achieving the goal of power.

> *"The first step is to get all of the ingredients out on the counter. We just picked our beautiful home-grown tomatoes, so we'll definitely want to use those. And we'll need some fresh spinach, lettuce, an orange, feta cheese, shelled walnuts…"*

4. **Demonstrate.** Show your child how to perform the skill, explaining slowly as you do.

> *"Now we need to whisk the salad dressing to mix all the ingredients together, like this … See how gently I'm whisking? That's so it won't splash."*

5. **Let your child try.** Let your child perform the skill while you stand by, ready to offer help if he needs it. Be gentle about mistakes.

> *"OK, now you try whisking. Very gently … that's it."*

6. **Encourage, encourage, encourage.** Make plenty of encouraging comments that acknowledge your child's efforts and results. This builds self-esteem and keeps his motivation high to continue learning.

   "Nice job! You have a knack for this!"

7. **Work or play together.** Once your child has learned the skill, you can sometimes work or play together, so that you can both enjoy the companionship of the activity.

   "And now we've really worked up an appetite, so let's eat!"

When we take these steps to teach our children new skills, work and play together, and simply take time to quietly enjoy each other's company, we strengthen our family and move toward a greater understanding of one another. So it goes with God. We can build and strengthen our relationship with God when we spend quiet time in prayer and seek wisdom from Holy Scripture, which is replete with instructions for daily living and guidance directly from God:

> **"These commands that I give you today are to be upon your hearts. Impress them on your children. Talk about them when you sit at home and when you walk along the road, when you lie down and when you get up."**
>
> *Deuteronomy 6:6-8 (NIV)*

Impress. Talk. Sit. Walk. Lie down. Get up. These words tell us to put our faith into action in our homes in order to protect and prepare our children with God's loving grace to survive and thrive in the society in which we live, following the example of Jesus Christ through the power of the Holy Spirit. Remember, God is an Active Parent.

6: Active Parenting for Unity & School Success

When talking to parents, especially parents of spirited children, a cartoon comes to mind. It depicts two men meeting each other for the first time. Both men look like they have just gone twelve rounds with a grizzly bear and lost badly. Their hair is disheveled, clothing torn, and they have similar hang-dog expressions on their weary faces. Behind them, written on a blackboard, are the words, Parent-Teacher Night. One of the men is introducing himself, as the caption reads: "You must be Timmy's dad. I'm Timmy's teacher."

When people see this cartoon, they always respond the same way. They laugh very hard. They get it. But there is more to this than the obvious joke. It is clear from the cartoon that both of these men share a similar problem named Timmy. What is less clear is if they understand that they share a common goal: to help Timmy survive and thrive in the kind of society in which he lives. Right now they are not succeeding in this goal. But if they can find a way to cooperate with each other, their chances for turning things around are excellent.

Scripture can help us see the importance of cooperation on a much larger scale.

> "God has placed the parts in the body, every one of them …
> The eye cannot say to the hand, 'I don't need you!'
> And the head cannot say to the feet, 'I don't need you!'
> On the contrary … there should be no division in the body,
> but … its parts should have equal concern for each other.
> If one part suffers, every part suffers with it;
> if one part is honored, every part rejoices with it.
> Now you are the body of Christ, and each one of you is a part of it."
>
> *1 Corinthians 12:18-21, 25-27 (NIV)*

This passage tells us that all of humankind is one body. Just as God designed the parts of a human body to work together and function as one, God designed humans to support one another and work together to bring Christ's presence alive in the world. It is God's will that we work in unity with others to raise our children, and in so doing we can provide everything they need to survive and thrive. A good education is one of these things, and many parents are concerned about being able to ensure it for their children.

The purpose of this chapter is to help you build on the skills you have been learning in this book to help your child succeed in school. We will often return to the concepts of cooperation and unity, because our children's education is a group effort. It involves parents, teachers, peers, family members, and others who are active in our children's lives, all working together toward the common goal of providing the best education possible. Sure, we all know stories of successful men and women who have done well in life in spite of doing poorly in school. They have gotten it together, beaten the odds, and deserve to be congratulated. The problem is that so many others do not. Without a good education, they find that the deck is stacked against them. They may still survive in spite of this, but it is unlikely that they will ever really thrive. This, by the way, is as true for the children of financially well-off families as it is for children of poorer families.

Active Parents take education seriously. Christian Active Parents use their faith to enhance their children's education. They understand that it is about more than just grades; it is about developing an appetite for learning. When a child's curiosity is sparked, when she gets real pleasure from discovering something she did not know, or reading a poem that moves her emotionally, or experiencing the joy of the "a-ha" moment when it all comes together and she "gets it," or creating something with her own hands and mind that never existed before, a child has a good chance of becoming a lifelong learner. She has a good chance of joyfully thriving.

There are many things you can do to help this special process happen. We're going to talk about seven of them.

Seven Smart Things Christian Active Parents Do to Help Their Children Succeed in School

Smart Thing #1: Show up and show support.

> "Let us not give up meeting together, as some are in the habit of doing, but let us encourage one another — and all the more as you see the Day approaching."
>
> *Hebrews 10:25 (NIV)*

There are lots of things that contribute to a child's success in school, and there have been lots of studies done to determine which are the most important. They considered many different factors, such as:

- Quality of the teachers, school leadership, and other staff

- School facilities

- Curriculum

- Educational level of the child's parents

- Income of the child's family

- Parents' involvement in the child's learning

The factor that over two hundred studies have labelled as the most important is "parents' involvement in the child's learning." When parents get involved both at home and at school, these studies show that their child is more likely to:

- Get better grades

- Do better on standardized tests

- Have higher attendance rates

- Graduate and go on to college

- Be involved in extracurricular activities

- Feel more connected to the school

- Have higher self-esteem and better behavior

Parent involvement means a lot of things, but first it means showing up at school and showing your support. Make a point to be there for Parent-Teacher night and conferences with your child's teacher. Look for opportunities to volunteer. Get to know other parents. Be there for school plays and other special activities when you can. If you have work conflicts, talk to your employer about reworking your schedule around important school events. Being involved in your child's school life will both keep you informed and bring you closer to your child, all the while shepherding that child to success. For as Proverbs 27:23 (NIV) encourages: "Be sure you know the condition of your flocks, give careful attention to your herds."

Who knows, you may find that you go beyond just being involved. You may actually become engaged in your child's learning. You might find yourself on committees that help move your school forward and otherwise contribute to the overall growth and development of the entire school community. Regardless of whether you had a good school experience as a child or hated every minute of it, your support now matters. You matter. And most quality schools (or schools that want to become quality schools) want you there, as involved or engaged as your time allows.

Smart Thing #2: Get to know your child's teachers and encourage them.

Everybody needs encouragement, and teachers are no exception. In fact, they could probably use a little extra encouragement and will appreciate it. There are also benefits to encouraging your child's teacher. First, when a teacher feels supported by her students' parents, she feels better about herself, her job, and her mission to help educate students. This makes her a better teacher for your kids. Second, people tend to feel more positive toward those who make them feel good about themselves. Encouragement does that. When you establish a positive relationship with your child's teacher, she is naturally going to be a little more sensitive to your child's needs.

When you take an interest in others, you are recognizing their significance and showing that you value them.

Make a point of getting to know your child's teachers. This in itself is encouraging. When you take an interest in others, you are recognizing their significance and showing that you value them. Take the opportunity at open houses and parent-teacher meetings to ask them about themselves before jumping into academics. Remember that teachers are people like you. They like to share with people they find supportive and genuinely interested in them. Be one of those people and you will find that everybody comes out ahead.

Other ways you might encourage your child's teacher include:

■ Let them know what you appreciate about them. For example:

> *"I really appreciate how hard you work to make school interesting for the students. I wish you had been my second grade teacher!"*

> *"Thanks for letting Ben do his comedy routine for five minutes at the end of class last week. That was so nice of you. He loved it!"*

■ Let them know that you value what they do. For example:

> *"I think it's great that you're a teacher. We need more teachers like you, teachers who really care about kids and who they become."*

> *"Your dedication to your students is such a blessing. Every day I thank God for sending us such a great teacher."*

■ Show confidence in them. For example:

> *"I'm not sure how we can solve this problem right now, but I know that between us we will come up with something good for Carl."*

> *"I have a feeling that this is going to be a great year!"*

■ Write them a letter (or e-mail) of encouragement. For example:

> Dear Betty,
>
> I just wanted to take a moment to thank you for all the help that you have given Michael this year. He has been learning so much, and I know how much time and effort you have put into the class. Maybe more important, you have such a special way of nurturing the kids. Thanks to you, they are not only becoming better students, but better people, as well.
>
> Thank you so much!
>
> Mona Popkin

Even if you aren't as crazy about your child's teacher as Michael was about Miss Betty Hickman, his second grade teacher, you can still find positive things to write or say. Just be truthful, specific, and sincere.

Smart Thing #3: Make learning a family priority.

**"Intelligent people are always ready to learn.
Their ears are open for knowledge."**

Proverbs 18:15 (NLT)

School success is about a lot more than just what goes on at school. It begins with the atmosphere you develop in your home about learning. It continues when your family is out in the community. And then it carries over into the classrooms and school building itself. Making sure your kids know that learning is a priority in your family will not only foster an attitude that helps them do better in school, it will help them do better later in life, too. After all, we live in a society that is changing so rapidly that it is likely your children will need to continue learning their entire lives just to keep up. Teaching them that learning is an important and enriching part of everyday life will help them do that and get more out of it.

Making sure your kids know that learning is a priority in your family will not only foster an attitude that helps them do better in school, it will help them do better later in life, too.

There are a lot of ways to make learning a priority in your family. Try some of these, and come up with more with your family:

- Model the joy of of learning throughout your life by taking courses, attending Bible studies, reading both fiction and nonfiction books, using the Internet, television, and other media to learn and discover (as well as for pleasure), and encouraging your children to take part when you can.

- Take turns bringing an interesting article or news item to the dinner table and have a family discussion about it. (Rose Kennedy used to do this with her family every evening at dinner, and she raised a U.S. president and three senators.) In the same vein, read a passage aloud from the Bible and discuss it over dinner with your family.

- Take your children to museums, historical landmarks, libraries, and other places where learning will occur naturally. Then look for ways to make it fun and interesting.

- Find creative ways to combine learning with entertainment and recreational activities. For example, take a hike as a family and ask the kids to find the most unusual thing they can in nature. Go to a ball game and then go online to see if the players and team did better or worse than their averages.

- Develop a "work before play" philosophy in your family. In other words, when there is a conflict between schoolwork (or chores) and something fun, schoolwork is the first priority. Exceptions can be made, but the key is an attitude that work is vitally important, not because parents demand it, but because the culture demands it.

- Limit TV watching and other "screen time" for everyone in the family, especially during homework time. Play games together and look for other creative ways to have fun.

- Complement your kids on how they use their minds more than their ability to play a sport, look good, or be popular. A mother of a very successful woman, who also happened to be very beautiful, once attributed her success to the fact that when she was a child and someone would tell her mother how pretty she was, her mother always added, "and smart as a whip" to the complement.

Smart Thing #4: Structure homework time.

Kids like homework about as much as teachers like grading tests, which is to say, not much. It's just part of the job and successful students, and good teachers, manage to get it done and done well. There has been a lot of controversy surrounding homework recently, and many schools are taking a second look at how much and what kind of homework they require. Some research even suggests that homework itself may be of limited benefit for elementary school students and only really pays off in high school. Others suggest that practice assignments improve scores on class tests at all grade levels and that a little homework may help elementary school students build good study habits.

One standard that many school districts are turning to is the "10-minute rule" created by Duke University psychology professor Harris Cooper. The rule, endorsed by the National PTA and the National Education Association, says kids should get 10 minutes of homework a night per grade. A first grader would have 10 minutes of homework each night; a fifth grader would have 50 minutes.

The following suggestions can help your child get the most out of homework and do better at school.

1. Help your child set up a regular work area.

Christian Active Parents allow freedom within limits, knowing when to step in and help and when to back off and just support.

Dictator and Doormat parents get it partly right. Dictators recognize that children need their parents to participate in their educations, but these parents go too far and become over-involved. Doormats recognize that school is a child's job and to do it well, children need the freedom to make choices and mistakes along the way, but these parents back off too far and don't show enough support.

Christian Active Parents allow freedom within limits, discerning with God's guidance when to step in and help and when to back off and just support. They focus their attention on helping their child

223

choose a regular work area where they can develop a good homework habit. Making it "regular" will help cue the child that it is time to work, not play. Whether it is a desk in his room, his bed (for reading, not writing or typing), or the kitchen table does not matter as long as it is quiet. Kids have their own preferences about studying and that is okay as long as they are able to concentrate and get the work done. Some prefer background music, others like quiet. This does not seem to matter, with the exception of TV or loud, distracting music, both of which have been found to interfere with concentration.

2. Agree on a regular study time.

Applying our CAP theme of "freedom within limits," we want to help our children develop a good homework habit by choosing a regular time for study. Some kids may prefer to get it done right after they get home from school while others may want time to play or relax before diving in to more schoolwork. The key is to make the time as regular as possible, knowing that flexibility will be called for when special events interfere.

Keep in mind your child's energy needs and do not make homework time run into bedtime if your child gets tired late in the day. We also recommend that you continue a work before play philosophy when it comes to watching TV or other entertainment. If your child wants a break from school before doing homework, that's a good time for physical activity or creative play — not "vegging out." If you have more than one child of homework age, try to schedule homework for the same time for everyone, if possible. This will help create a positive homework atmosphere and fewer distractions.

Talk with your child's teacher (or ask at parent-teacher night) about how much time to allow for homework. Schedule this amount of time on a regular basis, whether or not he has homework on a given night. On those nights he can use the study time on school related activities. This policy will help keep him from rushing through homework and help build up the homework habit. If your child often needs extra time to finish, use your active communication skills from Chapter 2 to talk with your child about the problem. If you cannot solve the problem together, then let the teacher know.

3. Make it a quiet learning time for all family members.

One way to reinforce how much you value school success is to make sure that the house is reasonably quiet during homework time. When the TV is blaring or others are making lots of noise, it can be a real distraction for some children. Have a short family meeting in order for everyone to agree on a "quiet time" or "learning time" for the entire family. This is a great time for parents to model the importance of learning by reading a book or article, completing Bible study homework, or engaging in some other quiet learning activity.

4. Develop a homework "to do" list.

One of the most powerful time management tools ever invented is the "to do" list. The simple process of writing down assignments and then checking them off as they are completed will help your child succeed at school and in dozens of other situations. Talk with your child about how she would like to do this (e.g. write in a notebook, use an electronic device, etc.) and then check to encourage her progress in following through. The key is to be consistent. Again, this develops a good habit. Plus, writing it down takes the pressure off of memory. Not only does this reduce anxiety about something "falling through the cracks," but the process of checking off items as you complete them is a great encouragement for doing homework.

Coaching Your Kids for Academic Success

The 21st-century world in which your child will live and work will place less value on reciting facts and more on thinking, communicating, problem-solving, cooperating in teams, and applying concepts in meaningful ways. Of course knowing factual information will still be important, but with computers and search engines able to sift through vast amounts of information at incredible speeds, the human's job will be to use that information creatively, think critically, and stay motivated. Schools are adapting to these changes, and parents can help by coaching their kids along these lines.

Although you may not be a teacher, you can help your children in school through positive coaching. Keep these seven principles in mind:

1. **Be available.** Don't do it for them, but offer support and guidance if needed.

2. **Offer encouragement, not criticism.** Find something positive to say before pointing out errors. Never, ever, ever attack the child's personality.

3. **Focus on effort instead of grades.** The grades will come.

4. **You don't have to be an expert to help.** Don't be afraid to say, "I don't know."

5. **Don't expect perfection.** The goal is improvement, not perfection. Focus your attention on helping your child improve, step by step, and he will eventually succeed. Focus your attention on perfection, and he will eventually say ugly things about you to a therapist.

6. **Turn the thinking over to the child.** Don't fall into the trap of doing the work for your child. Let her struggle a little bit for the answer and enjoy the success of getting it herself.

7. **Enjoy!** Demonstrate the joy of learning by smiling, laughing, and basking in each other's company. If all else fails, bake cookies.

Smart Thing #5: Read and talk with your child.

You may have heard that reading aloud to your child is the best way to improve reading skills. This is true. You may have also heard that reading skills are the best predictor of current and future school success. This is also true. But did you know that reading skills are also the best predictor of algebra skills and success in college? How about that they are the best predictor of future career success and earning power? Research supports this as well. Reading is the key to learning almost anything, and our schools are heavily geared toward rewarding good readers.

One of the best things you can do to improve your child's chances to survive and thrive in our communication-based society is to read to your child and engage her in conversation.

Clearly, one of the best things you can do to improve your child's chances of surviving and thriving in our communication-based society is to read to your child and engage her in conversation. When you read aloud to your child, all kinds of good things happen. When children feel free to simply listen to stories, they can focus on the plot, language patterns, and new vocabulary words more completely than they can when they are focusing on figuring out the words themselves. Remember that Jesus Himself was a storyteller, using parables to teach many of His most important truths. Reading Bible stories aloud to our children can teach lifelong lessons and values, helping them to walk in the ways of the Lord and create a living faith within.

Reading aloud to children also exposes them to more complex books than they can read independently, encouraging them to want to become better readers. It is also a wonderful bonding activity. As you cuddle together to explore new worlds of mystery and suspense, you open doors that spark the curiosity and thoughtfulness that are the essence of learning. Keep in mind these keys to building a strong reading foundation:

Read aloud to your child every day. Start this daily habit as soon as your child's eyes can focus on the pictures, or earlier if you like. As kids get older, they can read to you, or you can pick books that are too advanced for them and read them aloud or listen to the audio book together. A good goal is to read together 20 minutes daily. You may want to split this time between reading a children's book and reading a Bible story or other Christian material. And though bedtime is often the best time to read together, it's by no means the only time. For instance, you could read an age appropriate devotional aloud to your children in the morning while they wait for their ride to school. This is a great way to teach them about God's involvement in our lives on a daily basis.

Demonstrate that reading can be fun. Improving your child's reading skills is one goal of reading together. Another goal is to help your child become a lifelong reader, a habit that will pay off in better grades, better jobs, and a richer life. To accomplish this, begin by finding reading material that is interesting to your child, not you. Then make reading time fun: laugh together, make jokes, cuddle, and share the emotions of the book together. Go to the library and pick out books together or go online and download them. Whatever works for you and your budget is fine. Finally, let your child catch you reading for pleasure on your own. This models that reading is not only school "work," but also everyday fun.

Let your child catch you reading for pleasure on your own. This models that reading is not only school "work," but also everyday fun.

Pause in your reading to share or ask questions. You can share what you think about a character or event in the story, or you can explain the ideas, pictures, questions, and connections that go through your mind as you read. For example, if you read the sentence, "The black stallion was the most beautiful horse she had ever seen," you might pause and talk about the picture of the horse that you have in your mind or describe a beautiful horse that you once saw or rode. Then ask your child to share the picture or memory the words created in his mind. This helps develop analytical thinking skills and reading comprehension, and it teaches how a good reader interacts with a book. Here are some other ways to do this:

- Reinforce memory by asking your child what happened in the last segment you read together.

- Encourage observation by asking who, what, where, and when questions during the story or after the end of a short story.

- Help your child learn to think ahead by asking her to predict what might happen next.

- Develop language skills by asking the meaning of unusual words and discussing them or looking them up together.

- Ask why he thinks the author had the character do what he did.

- Build self-esteem and a love for learning by offering encouragement when your child answers these questions.

Encourage language development by talking and listening to each other. Closely related to reading to your child is the simple art of conversation. Most families spend too much time watching others talk on TV, movies, the Internet, and other media outlets, and not enough time practicing this age-old skill themselves. Use time spent driving places, mealtime, waiting for the food to come out in a restaurant, and other opportunities to talk about whatever topics your child shows an interest in, including the book you are currently reading together. A few ideas may help you engage your child:

- Ask open-ended questions instead of "yes" or "no" questions. For example:

  "What did you like about school today?

"Who did something funny today? What happened?"

"What do you think about when you are thinking about 'nothing'?"

■ Share about something that happened in the news and ask your child what she thinks about it.

■ Make up stories together, taking turns adding parts.

Smart Thing #6: Filter *in* the positive and *out* the negative.

We live in a time of exploding connectivity. The Internet links people all over the world. Every day, new websites and software, including social media sites, games, and apps, give us more and better ways to connect with one another. More advanced devices and ways to use these resources are emerging all the time. Not only has connectivity become an important part of how we learn and interact with others, but it is also integral to how we live. For children to succeed today, they must be able to use technology and media skillfully.

Christian Active Parents filter and limit what they can, but they realize that the best filter is the child's own brain. So they also teach their children how to make good decisions for themselves.

On the other hand, there are real risks involved in opening the world of adults to our children. Media — TV shows, movies, videos, photos, podcasts, music, games, websites — is more accessible than ever before. Though it benefits children in many ways, it can also influence their values in ways that are often unhealthy. Sexual and violent content is often just a click away. Predators roam the Internet looking to take advantage of overly trusting people, often the young and the elderly. Cyber bullies hide behind the anonymity of the web, looking for opportunities to strike out against others. Children post comments and pictures on websites without thinking about where they might end up and for how long they will be out there.

Christian Active Parents filter and limit what they can, but they realize that the best filter is the child's own brain. So they also teach their children how to make good decisions for themselves. God lives at the center of each one of us; there is no better filter for our children than God's Holy Spirit alive in their hearts. As Christians, we have a duty to make sure our children learn to recognize the Holy Spirit within them and tap into it through prayer, reading the Word of God, and connecting to the positive influence of a Christian community. Teaching our children from an early age to filter their life experiences through the wisdom of the Holy Spirit will provide guidance for them throughout their lives.

Spheres of Influence

As Christians, we want to make sure that our children learn from those who share our Christian heritage and beliefs. The realm of Christian influences is wide and varied. Picture your child's influences as a series of concentric circles with God at the center. We recognize God as the positive influence beyond all others. The next circle outside of God is for the influences of family, school, church, friends — in other words, all the people and institutions in your child's life. And the outermost circle is the realm that includes TV, the Internet, music, video games, and other forms of media. Just as you would protect your child from dangerous people and situations, you want to do what you can to screen out potentially harmful messages from this realm of media influences.

Child's Spheres of Influence

Movies · Internet · Family · Pastor/Priest · Friends · GOD · Caregivers · Youth Group Leaders · TV · Teachers · Other Media

Here are some suggestions for helping your child learn to use the Internet and other media safely and effectively:

- **Spend time online with your child.** If you don't have Internet access at home, check with your local library. They often have computers you can use for free. If you're not familiar with computers or the Internet, ask the librarian for help or see if there is a course available to help you and your child learn together. If your child knows more about Internet technology than you do, let her teach you. Ask her to explain what she is doing and why. Ask her to show you her favorite websites and apps and to tell you what she likes about them. This will help build her self-confidence and is a good family enrichment activity.

- **Help your child find useful websites.** Point her towards sites that can help her with homework or that relate to her interests. Use the Internet together to plan family trips, look up local activities, get information, research Scripture verses, and explore the world.

- **Pay attention to any games, apps, or other media she downloads.** Talk with him about the need to avoid games that are overly violent or sexual or contain other content that is unhealthy for children. Use rating codes to help you decide what is okay and what is off-limits.

- **Use filters to block your child from accessing sites that may be harmful.** These filters include software that you can install on your computer. In addition, many Internet service providers offer filters (often for free) that restrict the sites that children can visit. Be aware that filters are not always completely effective, and sometimes children can find ways around them. The best safeguard is your supervision and involvement.

■ **Monitor the amount of time that your child spends online.** Internet surfing can be just as absorbing as watching TV, or maybe even more so. Don't let it take over your child's life.

■ **Develop a clear set of guidelines for using the Internet.** Do this together at a family meeting, encouraging input from everyone. Then post these guidelines in your child's room and at least one public area. For example:

Our Family Internet Guidelines

For our own safety and the safety of other family members, we agree to these guidelines:

- We will not tell <u>anyone</u> — including friends — our computer passwords.

- We will not use bad language or send cruel, threatening, or untrue e-mails or text messages.

- We will not give out personal information to anyone we don't know in real life. This includes our own name, family members' names, home address, phone number, age, or school info (name, mascot, colors, etc.).

- We will not arrange to meet a stranger that we have talked with online.

- We will not post or e-mail pictures or videos of ourselves that we would not want our parents, boss, or other people now or in the future to see.

Smart Thing #7: Support your school's discipline plan.

Imagine how frustrating and chaotic it would be to play a game like basketball or soccer without having rules and people to enforce those rules. Organizations need rules, too. Whether it's a small family or a large corporation or even a country, without rules, conflicts get worse rather than better until the entire system breaks. Schools are no different. Without a clear set of rules to help students know what's expected, they can't succeed. And without knowing those rules, and being willing to follow them, your child can't succeed.

The seventh Smart Thing that Christian Active Parents do to support their child's success at school is to make sure everyone in the family knows the rules and supports them. In the best case, the school's rules and the family's rules are similar. But even when you disagree with part of the school's policy, it's smart to teach your child to follow it anyway — and then engage with other parents to work within the system and change it. Get a copy of the school's discipline plan and have a family talk to review and discuss it.

Tobacco, Alcohol, and Other Drugs: A Family Talk

It's particularly important to discuss the rules regarding violence (including bullying) and the use of tobacco, alcohol, and other drugs.

In fact, it's a good idea to have a family talk about these topics. The following dialogue is an example of how one family did just this. It is taken from a family talk in the *Christian Active Parenting* program video. As you read the dialogue, think about what you like about how the parents handle the talk and what you might do differently when you have a talk like this in your own family.

Family Talk: Tobacco, Alcohol, and Other Drugs

Ten-year-old Jordan and his parents, Jeffrey and Nicole, are seated around the dining room table.

Jeffrey: *Let's say a word of prayer before we begin. Dear Lord, guide our discussion as we consider this important subject of tobacco, alcohol, and other drugs. Help us to teach Jordan how to take care of the body you gave him and to keep him safe in a world in which too many of your children are being hurt by drugs. Thank you for blessing us with this time together. Amen.*

Jordan and Nicole: Amen

Jeffrey: *We called this meeting to talk about three of the biggest problems that kids face today: tobacco, alcohol, and other drugs.*

Jordan: *Drugs?*

Jeffrey: *Sure. This is something all families need to talk about — especially with so many movies and other types of entertainment showing this stuff looking cool or funny. And your school has a very clear policy against students using drugs.*

Nicole: *Here — I looked up the school's discipline policy on their website. Let's go over it, and then we want to hear what you think.*

Narrator: *The "family talk" is a type of meeting that serves to help children handle upcoming challenges with knowledge, courage, and integrity. Among these challenges, the risk of our kids using tobacco, alcohol, and other drugs is high on all our lists. Talking about them early can help lay a good foundation for later, when your child will be tempted to try them. Be sure to find out your child's school's policy about this, and include it in your talk. Four simple guidelines will help you make the most of your family talks:*

First, plan your introduction and the key points you want to cover. It's a good idea to plan a simple opening statement, like the one Jeffrey just used, to introduce the topic.

Our second guideline is to use open-ended questions to stimulate discussion. A family talk is meant to be a discussion, not a lecture, so it's important that you ask good questions and use Active Communication to listen and respond to children's answers.

Nicole: *To begin with, what do you already know about why tobacco, alcohol, and other drugs are so dangerous?*

Jordan: *(shrugs)*

Nicole: *We're really interested in what you think, Jordan, so help us out. What have you learned about this in school? And why do you think your school has a strict policy against them?*

Jordan: *Well, I know drugs can kill you…*

Nicole: *That's right. We've all heard about people who died from a drug overdose, drinking and driving, or a disease caused by smoking. So any of that stuff can kill you. What else?*

Jordan: *Drugs can make you do really weird stuff.*

Jeffrey: *Good point. Drugs affect the brain in ways that interfere with normal thinking. People under that influence are quicker to get into fights, or wreck their car, or just say and do really dumb things that seem cool while they are high.*

Narrator:	By encouraging your child's participation, you show that you respect him and want to hear his ideas, and this makes it much more likely that your message will get through. But make sure you follow **our third family talk guideline, which is to avoid communication blocks.** That means not criticizing, judging, preaching, or otherwise saying or doing something that will shut down the conversation.
Jordan:	But don't drugs make you feel good?
Nicole:	And that's the problem, isn't it? Drugs may make people feel good … at first. But the next day, when they have a really bad hangover, or down the road when they've gotten addicted, they can really get in a lot of trouble.
Jeffrey:	That's the truth. In the long run drugs can cause a lot more pain than pleasure.
Jordan:	Then why do you and Mom drink?
Jeffrey:	Well, keep in mind that drinking is legal for adults but not for kids. That's because when you're still growing, alcohol can interfere with healthy brain development. Even for adults, though, it's not smart to drink too much. Have you ever seen your mother and I getting drunk or using illegal drugs at all?
Jordan:	No. (laughing)
Jeffrey:	And you won't. Adults who do that are abusing their bodies and risking their health.
Jordan:	I know a kid whose parents let his big brother smoke cigarettes and drink beer sometimes.
Narrator:	When Jeffrey and Nicole allow their son to express his own thoughts, they show him that they value open communication. This helps set the stage for **our fourth guideline: share your values persuasively.**
Jeffrey:	Yes, some families may not really be aware of the dangers. But let's be clear that in our family, it's never okay for kids to drink or smoke — not even a little bit. And it's never okay for anybody at any age to use illegal drugs. This is pretty similar to your school's policy, so if you follow our family rules, you'll be okay at school, too.
Nicole:	I know that a lot of kids feel pressure to experiment with drugs because the older kids are doing them. It takes courage and character to do the right thing and say no.
Jeffrey:	And it also takes practice. Maybe we should talk about some ways that you can say no without feeling foolish. What would you say if someone offered you a cigarette?
Narrator:	The Moores continue asking questions and practicing what Jordan might do in tough situations, but they are careful not to let the conversation go on too long.
	Don't feel that you have to provide all the information yourself. In fact, **our fifth guideline is to find support materials.** By using articles, videos, and the Internet, you can provide more information in an interesting way. And of course, you will want to follow up on any materials you use with more discussion.
Jeffrey:	This has been a great talk, and you've had a lot of good ideas. Since there is so much more to know about this subject, we thought you might want to watch a short video we found online. Then we can talk about it.

In the dialogue, the Narrator mentioned five guidelines for conducting family talks:

Family Talk Guidelines

1. Plan your introduction and key points.

2. Use open-ended questions to stimulate discussion.

3. Avoid communication blocks.

4. Share your values persuasively.

5. Find support materials.

Trouble at School

What should you do if your child breaks a rule and you get called in to discuss the problem? While no parent wants to get a call like this, sometimes kids make poor decisions at school, just as they sometimes do at home or other places. If you are notified about such a problem or even asked to come in and discuss the situation, here are some tips that may help:

- Stay calm. Getting angry at your child or the school is likely to make the problem worse, not better.

- Treat it like any other parenting problem, using the problem solving model and skills you have been learning.

- Use Active Communication to talk to your child about what happened, how he felt, and how to handle the problem.

- Talk with him about taking the problem to God and asking forgiveness.

■ Use it as a learning opportunity for your child. Help him understand what he did wrong. Adding a logical consequence of your own to the school's discipline may be a good part of the lesson. For example, if the school calls for a suspension, find some meaningful work for your child to do while serving that suspension (while foregoing video games and other fun activities).

■ Discuss how he could apologize to the people who were hurt by his actions and ask them for forgiveness.

■ Avoid the temptation to rescue your child from the consequences of his actions, to blame the school, or otherwise undermine the learning opportunity. (If you and your child genuinely feel that he is being treated unfairly, then work to appeal the discipline through the proper channels.)

When you put the "Seven Smart Things" into action in your family, you send a loud and clear message to your children that education is important, that you care how they do in school, and that you want to help. Kids who get that message will have a leg up not only in school, but also at work, in their relationships, and throughout their lives.

Parents as Magnets: Encouraging Positive Events

If parents can filter out certain negative events that might harm or negatively influence our children, we can also attract or encourage positive events that can help build the character that leads to a success cycle. As much as we might like to think otherwise...

No child gets everything he needs from his parents.

Children have to supplement what their parents give them with information from other adults and peers. You can help this process along by thinking of creative ways to introduce positive influences into your child's life. Here are a few types of influences to consider:

Positive Adult Influences

Make sure that your child has positive contact with other adult mentors, such as youth group leaders, pastors and other faith leaders, coaches, teachers, relatives, especially grandparents and others without young children of their own, and adults from mentoring programs such as Big Brother/Big Sister.

Since children do not usually choose their own adult influences, it is up to parents to do what they can to make sure the adults in their children's lives have the values and character to be good influences. This does not mean that they must be Christians or share your beliefs about all things. Children can learn from all people of good will and positive values. Get to know the people who lead your children as much as possible and talk with your kids about what those leaders say and do when they are together. Be supportive and encouraging, but keep your eyes and ears open for signs of potential trouble.

Media

There are many positive role models and lessons in books, movies, music, TV, and the Internet. Help your child find and take advantage of this positive input and you will strengthen many positive values. Watch movies or TV shows together and talk about the lessons being taught. While driving, tune into a Christian radio station as part of your listening habits. Be aware of current events and discuss pertinent issues around the dinner table. Integrating faith into family conversations will help your children notice how God is intricately involved and powerfully active in the world around them.

Summer Experiences

Summer camp can be a wonderful influence on children's development. Camp counselors and other staff often make excellent role models. There are many kinds of camp to choose from, including sports camps, academic camps, camps for musicians, horse lovers, sailing, and so on. Overnight camp gives children a chance to experience a degree of independence in a safe environment, providing opportunities to explore unique interests, develop special relationships with new friends and mentors, and make memories they'll recall fondly throughout their lives. Day camps can offer a variety of growth experiences, as well. Many churches have Vacation Bible School during the summer, a great way to enrich children's faith.

A Loving Spiritual Education

When delivered with love and support, a spiritual education provides positive lessons of character as well as faith. Choosing a church and attending services regularly, starting when your children are young, is a good place to begin. Church can have its greatest influence on our children when they view it as their second home. Attending Sunday school regularly allows them to learn Biblical truths and develop Christian friends, plus it establishes the habit of looking to the Bible and to other believers for support. Being part of a church community opens countless opportunities for a child, such as youth ministry, volunteer projects, youth choir, mission trips, and Bible studies — activities that help build strong character and encourage children to become actively invested in their faith. When spiritual education is positive and energizing, children will enjoy the habit of regular church attendance. As they see the benefits of this habit emerge in their lives, they will continue to feed their living faith as they grow to be adults.

A Good Academic Environment

Let's face it: all schools are not created equal. Your children will spend more time at school than any place other than their beds, so find the best one that your financial situation will allow, even if it means you have to move to a different location. The value of a good educational environment is more than just the sum of the its teachers and facilities. Just as important are the attitudes and values of your child's classmates and their families, as they can also have an enormous influence on your child.

The Importance of Family Meetings

Just as freedom of speech is a basic freedom in our democratic society, a cooperative household must allow its members the same freedom.

One of the themes stressed in CAP is the importance of allowing children a voice in decisions that affect their lives. Just as freedom of speech is a basic right in our democratic society, a cooperative household must allow its members the same freedom. By allowing children to influence our decisions through respectful discussion, we are actually better able to maintain our parental authority. Knowing that their voices and opinions make a difference builds cooperation and responsibility and makes anger and rebellion less likely. This is as true in the family as it is in society at large, and it is part of preparing our children to live and participate in the larger world. Holding regular family meetings is a good way to start.

Remember these words from Matthew 18:20 (NIV): "For where two or three gather in my name, there am I with them." Beginning a family meeting with prayer focuses everyone on the realization that God is present and actively involved in the family discussion.

There are different types of family meetings:

■ **Informal Meetings**
These are informal, quick meetings to make a decision about something affecting the family in the near future. In Chapter 1, we introduced this type of family meeting to decide on a family enrichment activity, "Taking Time for Fun." In Chapter 2, we talked about having a simple family meeting to set a bedtime routine.

■ **Problem-Prevention Talks**
We introduced this type of meeting in Chapter 3 as a method of anticipating and preventing problems before they happen.

■ **Character Talks**
Presented in Chapter 4, these are discussions aimed at building positive character traits and values in your children.

■ **Problem Solving Meetings Using the FLAC Method**
This type of meeting, presented in Chapter 5, uses the FLAC

method in a family meeting format to solve problems owned by parents, children, or shared.

■ **Family Council Meetings**

This is a more formal type of meeting that operates much like a business meeting. See Addendum III for a guide to introducing family council meetings in your family.

If you have not already begun using some of these types of family meetings in your own family, it's important that you make the effort to begin as soon as your children are old enough to participate (usually by about age seven). In case you are still not convinced, here are six more good reasons to hold family meetings:

1. **Faith.** Faith is a Christian family's firm foundation. When you take time to pray together and seek God's guidance on matters influencing your family, you teach your children that the Lord is actively involved in your daily challenges, relationships, and decisions.

2. **Cooperation.** Regular family meetings teach each person in the family that all are in the same boat, all on board can share in steering the boat, and the best way to decide how and where to steer it is to share feelings and opinions until an agreement is reached.

3. **Responsibility.** Regular participation in family meetings teaches each person in the family to make the best choices she can make on behalf of the family. After all, everyone will have to live with the consequences once the choices are made.

4. **Courage.** Family meetings are laboratories for individual courage. Each family member learns how important it is to say what he really thinks and feels, even if it isn't shared by anybody else. Meetings also provide opportunities for sharing encouragement.

5. **Mutual respect.** Family meetings are governed by one overriding rule: Everyone must treat each other with respect.

This means everything from listening while others are talking to not putting down anyone's idea's, feelings, or personality.

6. **Self-esteem.** When children see their ideas valued and their participation welcomed, they think well of themselves. This self-esteem can carry over into other aspects of their lives.

That these six qualities are the same character traits we said were essential for our children *to survive and thrive in the kind of society in which they will live* is no coincidence. After all, the society in which they will live is most likely to be democratic. Our purpose as parents is, once again, to prepare them to live successfully within it. Family meetings help prepare our children to be involved citizens and contributing members of their communities.

Family Enrichment Activity: Emphasizing Family Unity

Active Parenting believes that families are the backbone of civilization and that your family is the most important family in the world ... to your children.

Active Parenting believes that families are the backbone of civilization and that your family is the most important family in the world ... to your children. History has proven time after time that we could never survive alone, but by forming small cooperative units, we can thrive. Families have been a source of belonging, learning, and contribution for children and for society — and, to a large extent, the measure of any civilization rests on the strength of its families.

A hospice chaplain who has sat at the bedsides of hundreds of people in their final days, hours, and minutes of life wrote about what she had learned from her experience in a blog post. She found that when people know their death is near, they want to talk about the things that mean the most to them, and often that means they talk about their families and how well they loved and received love from them. This is how they talk about the meaning of their lives. In other words, it's how they talk about God.

What can the rest of us learn from this hospice chaplain's patients? Though we may spend a lot of time thinking about matters of the

Spirit, the real living of life happens in our families — both those we're born with and those we choose — and that is where we learn about love. Through loving relationships, we learn about God. So, although it is important to shepherd the growth of our children's faith by attending church, introducing them to scripture, and praying together, the best way we can teach them about God is to make family a haven of wholehearted, unconditional love.

So whether you are part of a traditional Mom-and-Dad family, a blended stepfamily, a single-parent family, or any other style of family, it's important to look for ways to let your children know that they are part of a family unit. Plan frequent family activities; use phrases like "in our family," and develop your own family traditions and rituals. And give your children the gift of memories by telling and retelling the special stories of your family's history that make your family unique.

Remember, too, that through your family, your children will learn that they belong to a much larger family, the family of humankind. And since their contributions to that family will help determine the future of all people, your job as a parent may very well be the most important job in the world.

Fortunately, we are not alone in this life-shaping endeavor. The love, encouragement, and guidance we give to our children are first given to us by God. As Christian Active Parents, we are empowered by the Lord to empower our children.

> **"Now follow the example of the correct teaching I gave you,**
> **and let the faith and love of Christ Jesus be your model.**
> **You have been trusted with a wonderful treasure. Guard it**
> **with the help of the Holy Spirit, who lives within you."**
>
> *2 Timothy 1:13-14 (CEV)*

"A child is a person who is going to carry on what you have started. He is going to sit where you are sitting, and when you are gone, attend to those things which you think are important. You may adopt all the policies you please, but how they are carried out depends on him. He will assume control of your cities, states, and nations. He is going to move in and take over your churches, schools, universities, and corporations. All your books are going to be judged, praised, or condemned by him. The fate of humanity is in his hands. **"**

–Abraham Lincoln

The Job of My Life

Lyrics to the Active Parenting Theme Song

Sometimes I wonder what to say
To make it better, to make it okay.
Sometimes I wonder just what to do,
Where to take a stand
And how to help them through
Through the tough times and the glad times,
The times we share as a family.
It's not long, the time we have together
Together as a family.
Active Parenting
The most important job in my life
Active Parenting
Helped me do the job of my life.
And so I'm giving it all I can.
I'm a special part of a special plan.
And joy is growing within my heart
For my precious child as we make this start.

Active Parenting
The most important job in my life
Active Parenting
Helped me do the job of my life.
Long ago, we didn't know
What challenges lay ahead.
But now the joy is real,
And it's such a different feel
To love this child with my eyes opened wide,
Learning more each day
About the Active Parenting way.
Active Parenting
The most important job in my life
Active Parenting
Helped me do the job of my life.

–Michael H. Popkin

Addendum I.
Alcohol, Tobacco, and Other Drugs:
Developing Protective Factors

Research over the past twenty years has shown that certain factors in a child's life can increase that child's risk for using and becoming addicted to alcohol, tobacco, and other drugs. The good news is that there are other "protective factors" that can help guard children against these risks. The more protective factors exist in a child's life, the less likely the child will use or abuse these substances.

The chart below details the protective factors in six domains of a child's life (left column) and presents ways that parents can help develop these factors in their children (right column). It also includes the Active Parenting skills that address each protective factor and the chapter(s) of this guide in which you can find them.

Parents can have the most influence in the Family domain, but as the chart shows, there are many ways to develop protective factors in the other domains as well. Read over the chart carefully and ask yourself:

- *How many of these actions am I already taking?*
- *How many of these actions could I start taking?*
- *How can I be more effective in developing these factors in my child?*

PROTECTIVE FACTORS	HOW PARENTS CAN HELP DEVELOP THEM
INDIVIDUAL DOMAIN	
Positive personal characteristics, including: social skills and social responsiveness; cooperation; emotional stability, positive sense of self; flexibility; problem-solving skills; and low levels of defensiveness	• Work to instill qualities of positive character in child (i.e. courage, responsibility, self-esteem, and respect). (All chapters, especially Ch. 1)
	• Encourage positive bonding with child. (Family Enrichment Activities, Ch. 1-6)
Bonding to societal institutions and values, including: attachment to parents and extended family; commitment to school; regular involvement with religious institutions; and belief in society's value	• Communicate expectations clearly; listen actively. (Active Communication, Ch. 2; Seven Smart Things, Ch. 6.)
	• Provide child with age-appropriate choices. (Method of Choice, Ch. 1)
Social and emotional competence, including: good communication skills, responsiveness; empathy; caring; sense of humor, inclination toward pro-social behavior; problem-solving skills; sense of autonomy; sense of purpose and of the future (e.g., goal-directedness); and self-discipline	• Help child solve problems he owns, and involve child in solving family problems. (Problem-Handling Model, Ch. 2; FLAC Method, Ch. 5)
	• Build on child's strengths; show confidence in child's ability. (Encouragement, Ch. 4)
	• Help child manage anger (Ch. 5)

PROTECTIVE FACTORS	HOW PARENTS CAN HELP DEVELOP THEM

FAMILY DOMAIN

Positive bonding among family members **Parenting that includes:** high levels of warmth and avoidance of severe criticism; sense of basic trust; high parental expectations; and clear and consistent expectations, including children's participation in family decisions and responsibilities **An emotionally supportive parental/family milieu, including:** parental attention to children's interests; orderly and structured parent-child relationships; and parent involvement in homework and school-related activities	• Express love and affection to child on a regular basis. Establish consistent routines. (Bedtime Routines and "I Love You"s, Ch. 2) • Use positive discipline methods. (Basic Discipline, Ch. 3) • Emphasize family unit. (Family Enrichment Activities, Ch.1-6) • Involve child in family decisions and responsibilities. (Family Meetings, All chapters; Preventing Problems, Ch. 3) • Encourage child in all areas, including school; Build on strengths.; Value child for who he/she is. (Encouragement, Ch. 4) • Communicate expectations clearly. (Active Communication, Ch. 2; Discipline, Ch. 3)

PEER DOMAIN

Association with peers who are involved in school, recreation, service, religion, or other organized activities	• Encourage positive peer relationships.; Provide opportunities to form positive peer relationships. (Parents as Magnets, Ch. 6)

SCHOOL DOMAIN

Caring and support, sense of "community" in classroom and school **High expectations from school personnel** **Clear standards and rules for appropriate behavior** **Youth participation, involvement, and responsibility in school tasks and decisions**	• Be involved in school activities; Be informed of what is happening in child's school; Know your child's teachers, Attend parent-teacher conferences. (Seven Smart Things, Ch. 6) • Show your child that learning and school are a priority; Read with your child regularly. (Seven Smart Things, Ch. 6) • Encourage your child in schoolwork and learning. (Encouragement, Ch. 4; Seven Smart Things, Ch. 6) • Build on child's strengths; Show confidence in child's ability. (Encouragement, Ch. 4; Teaching Skills, Ch. 5)

COMMUNITY DOMAIN

Caring and support **High expectations of youth** **Opportunities to participate in community activities**	• Seek out and provide opportunities for child to participate in positive community activities. (Parents as Magnets, Ch. 6) • Provide adult mentors in child's life. (Parents as Magnets, Ch. 6)

SOCIETY DOMAIN

Media literacy (resistance to pro-use messages) **Decreased accessibility** **Increased pricing through taxation** **Raised purchasing age and enforcement** **Stricter driving-under-the-influence laws**	• Monitor child's exposure to media. (Filtering Media, Ch. 6)) • Provide child with positive media exposure and limit negative exposure. (Filtering Media, Parents as Magnets, Ch. 6) • Discuss media issues with child, especially regarding ATODs; Listen actively to his point of view, and share yours convincingly. (Active Listening, Ch. 2; Filtering Media, Ch. 6) • Limit child's exposure to ATODs. (Parents as Filters, Ch. 6)

Addendum II.
The Search Institute's 40 Developmental Assets for Children

SUPPORT

1. **Family Support**
   Family life provides high levels of support.

2. **Positive Family Communication**
   Young people and their parent(s) communicate.

3. **Other Adult Relationships**
   Children have support from at least one adult other than their parents, and parents have support from people outside the home.

4. **Caring Neighborhood**
   Children experience caring neighbors.

5. **Caring Out-Of-Home Climate**
   School and other activities provide caring, encouraging environments for children.

6. **Parent Involvement in Out-of-Home Situations**
   Parents are actively involved in helping children succeed in school and in other situations outside the home.

EMPOWERMENT

7. **Community Values Children**
   Children feel that the family and community value and appreciate children.

8. **Children are Given Useful Roles**
   Children are included in age-appropriate family tasks and decisions and are given useful roles at home and in the community.

9. **Service to Others**
   Children serve others in the community with their family or in other settings.

10. **Safety**
    Children are safe at home, at school, and in the neighborhood.

BOUNDARIES AND EXPECTATIONS

11. **Family Boundaries**
    The family has clear rules and consequences and monitors children's activities and whereabouts.

12. **Out-of-Home Boundaries**
    Schools and other out-of-home environments provide clear rules and consequences.

13. **Neighborhood Boundaries**
    Neighbors take responsibility for monitoring children's behavior.

14. **Adult Role Models**
    Parents and other adults model positive, responsible behavior.

15. **Positive Peer Observation**
    Children interact with other children who model responsible behavior and have opportunities to plan and interact in safe, well-supervised settings.

16. **Appropriate Expectations for Growth**
    Adults have realistic expectations for children's development at this age.

CONSTRUCTIVE USE OF TIME

17. **Creative Activities**
    Parents, caregivers, other adults encourage children to achieve and develop their unique talents.

18. **Out-of-Home Activities**
    Children spend one hour or more each week in extracurricular school activities or structured community programs.

19. **Religious Community**
    The family attends religious programs or services for at least one hour per week.

20. **Positive, Supervised Time at Home**
    Children spend most evenings and weekends at home with their parents in predictable, enjoyable routines.

COMMITMENT TO LEARNING

21. Achievement Expectation and Motivation
Children are motivated to do well in school and other activities.

22. Children are Engaged in Learning
Children are responsive, attentive, and actively engaged in learning.

23. Stimulating Activity
Parents and teachers encourage children to explore and engage in stimulating activities. Children do homework when it's assigned.

24. Enjoyment of Learning and Bonding with School
Children enjoy learning and care about their school.

25. Reading for Pleasure
Children and an adult read together for at least 30 minutes a day. Children also enjoy reading or looking at books or magazines on their own.

POSITIVE VALUES

26. Caring
Children are encouraged to help other people.

27. Equality and Social Justice
Children begin to show interest in making the community a better place.

28. Integrity
Children begin to act on their convictions and stand up for their beliefs.

29. Honesty
Children begin to value honesty and act accordingly.

30. Responsibility
Children begin to accept and take personal responsibility for age-appropriate tasks.

31. Healthy Lifestyle and Sexual Attitudes
Children begin to value good health habits and learn healthy sexual attitudes and beliefs as well as respect for others.

SOCIAL COMPETENCIES

32. Planning and Decision Making Practice
Children begin to learn how to plan ahead and make choices at appropriate developmental levels.

33. Interpersonal Skills
Children interact with adults and children and can make friends. Children express and articulate feelings in appropriate ways and empathize with others.

34. Cultural Competence
Children know about and are comfortable with people of different cultural, racial, and/or ethnic backgrounds.

35. Resistance Skills
Children start developing the ability to resist negative peer pressure and dangerous situations.

36. Peaceful Conflict Resolution
Children try to resolve conflicts nonviolently.

POSITIVE IDENTITY

37. Personal Power
Children begin to feel they have control over things that happen to them. They begin to manage frustrations and challenges in ways that have positive results for themselves and others.

38. Self-Esteem
Children report having high self-esteem.

39. Sense of Purpose
Children report that their lives have purpose and actively engage their skills.

40. Positive View of Personal Future
Children are hopeful and positive about their personal future.

ADDENDUM III.
How to Hold a Family Council Meeting

The types of family meetings that we have previously discussed are useful methods of bringing your family together for specific, time-limited purposes. They may also be incorporated into the Family Council Meeting.

The Family Council Meeting offers an ideal forum for all family members to participate in resolving problems and making family decisions. This is a time, once a week, when the entire family gathers to make plans and handle problems that affect family members. It can last from 20 minutes to an hour and is conducted according to an agenda. In effect, it is what a business meeting is to an organization.

Your first Family Council Meeting should be a short one. It's an excellent idea to have only one item of business at this meeting and to plan an outing or a time for fun together afterwards. Later meetings can be longer and follow a more extensive agenda.

Suggested Agenda

Here is an agenda that works for many families. We will elaborate on it more in the section "How To Be an Effective Chairperson." You can modify it to fit your circumstances.

1. Compliments

2. Minutes

3. Old business/new business

4. Allowances

5. Treat or family activity

New Business Agenda

Most families find that the new business section of the family meeting works better if items have been written on a posted agenda before the meeting. A sheet of paper labeled "Agenda" can be taped to the refrigerator or posted at another convenient location. When a problem occurs that a family member would like handled at the next family meeting, she writes it on the agenda. For example:

NEW BUSINESS AGENDA

1. Why can't I spend the night with Melissa? -Sara

2. Sara keeps coming into my room without asking. -Jose

3. need help with chores. -Mom

Agenda items are handled in order at the next family meeting. Items that are not brought up before the meeting is over can be carried over to the next meeting. Many times, an agenda item will have been handled by those involved before the meeting and can be dropped from the list.

One final benefit of having a written agenda is that it offers parents an excellent way of staying out of children's fights. When a child tries to engage you in solving one of his problems, you can sympathetically suggest that it be put on the agenda for this week's meeting.

Nicholas: *"Daniel keeps taking my toys without asking. Tell him to stop."*

Mother: *"Gee, honey, you sound pretty angry about that. Why don't you put it on the agenda for this week's family meeting?"*

The ground rules for handling this type of problem during a family council meeting are exactly the same as during a problem-solving discussion using the FLAC method on pages 196 and 207.

Leadership Roles

There are two leadership roles at family meetings:

Chairperson: Keeps the discussion on track and sees that everybody's opinion is heard.

Secretary: Takes notes during the meeting, writes the minutes after the meeting, and reads the minutes at the next meeting.

These two duties can be assumed by the parents at the first meeting. After that, other family members should take turns being chairperson and secretary in an agreed-upon order, so that no one person is in charge every time.

How to Be an Effective Chairperson

Just follow the agenda:

1. **Compliments.** Ask if anyone appreciates something a family member said or did during the past week. This is a time for members of the family to say thanks to each other for good deeds and to encourage each other with compliments.

2. **Minutes.** Ask the person who was secretary last week to read the minutes aloud. The minutes remind everyone of what happened at the last meeting.

3. **Old business/new business.** Ask the family to talk about any matter that wasn't finished at the last meeting. These unfinished matters are called "old business." Let each person say what he or she wants to say, but remind people that they should not talk when someone else is talking.

   Next, ask the family to talk about matters that have been written on the agenda.

4. **Allowances.** This is a good time for Mom or Dad to pass out allowances.

5. **Treat or family activity.** End the meeting by saying, "The meeting is adjourned." People get tired if meetings go on too long, so keep your meeting to an agreed-upon time limit. We recommend 10-15 minutes with younger children (5- to 7-year-olds) and increasing to 30-45 minutes with older children. End on a positive note by doing something fun together. For example, play a game or have a dessert.

How to Be an Effective Secretary

To be an effective secretary, you need to do only three things:

1. Listen carefully to what is said.

2. Write down what is decided on each matter that is discussed.

3. Later (after the meeting), write a summary of what was decided. This summary is called "the minutes." Read the minutes aloud at the next meeting.

Here is what the minutes may look like:

Minutes of Family Meeting, March 14th

Chairperson was Jerry. Secretary was Linda. The family decided that:

1. We would go to Lake Lure this summer for vacation.

2. Jerry will pay Linda $10 for the lost ball.

3. We will wait until the next meeting to decide whether we want to go on the weekend hike in April with the hiking club.

The *Christian Active Parenting* Program

For Parents of Children Ages 5-12

This Parent's Guide is a component of the *Christian Active Parenting* video and discussion program, a parenting education course offered on a local level to parents and other caretakers of children. Participating in a "CAP" course is a fun, interesting, and effective way to learn the Christian Active approach to parenting. In each session, you will:

- Watch video vignettes modeling both positive parenting practices and methods you should avoid.

- An experienced group leader guides discussion and presents Active Parenting skills and theory.

- Discuss parenting issues with other parents in your group and provide mutual support and guidance.

- Participate in fun exercises that demonstrate concepts and teach Active Parenting skills.

…and much more!

To find a *Christian Active Parenting* course in your area, contact your local community center, church or other religious organization, hospital, mental health center, or other "helping professional" in your community.

If you are interested in starting your own *Christian Active Parenting* course, or if you would like to order additional copies of this book (quantity discounts available), call 800-825-0060. We'll be glad to guide you with help and resources as you strengthen parenting skills in your home, church, and community.

Visit the Active Parenting website for information about online courses, webinars, or the Online Video Library for *Christian Active Parenting* and many other parenting courses:

www.activeparenting.com